"As digital technologies penetrate into almost all products and services, they become more disruptive in every industry. Knowing that is easy; understanding and leading the required change is hard. *Digital to the Core* is a book that will help leaders find their pathways to success." —**DON TAPSCOTT, author of *Wikinomics* and, with Alex Tapscott, the forthcoming *Blockchain Revolution***

"Since leading a digital transformation in the airline industry, many C-level executives have asked me how they can generate similar transformation in their business. *Digital to the Core* lays down a solid framework with actionable takeaways for leaders to drive this change." —**GLENN MORGAN FBCS, Head of Digital Business Transformation, International Airlines Group**

"If the digital revolution has not yet hit your business, it soon will do. The authors argue the case for not just navigating digital business, but for embracing it, and offer helpful frameworks for all senior executives in rising to the challenge." —**MICHAEL EARL, Emeritus Professor of Information Management, Oxford University**

"It's too late to catch up with digital, but it's a great time to leapfrog. This book gives you practical clues about which way to jump." —**BOB JOHANSEN, author and Distinguished Fellow, Institute for the Future, Palo Alto, CA**

"Using the power of technology, the Internet, and the Internet of Things, new competition pops up from the most unexpected corner, requiring traditional companies to reinvent themselves to survive. This book provides excellent thought provocation and frameworks to start this journey towards a sustainable digital business." —**SABINE EVERAET, Europe Group CIO, The Coca-Cola Company**

"In *Digital to the Core*, the authors expertly challenge us to understand that never before have we grappled with strategic, cultural, and market force changes so significant. Every business model is being upended. Every customer expectation is rising to new heights. The digital revolution is underway and survival requires way more than surface level tactics." —**ROB CARTER, CIO, FedEx Corporation**

DIGITAL
TO THE
CORE

DIGITAL
TO THE
CORE

REMASTERING LEADERSHIP FOR
YOUR INDUSTRY,
YOUR ENTERPRISE,
AND YOURSELF

MARK RASKINO AND **GRAHAM WALLER**
GARTNER, INC.

bibliomotion
inc.

First published by Bibliomotion, Inc.
711 Third Avenue, New York, NY 10017, USA
2 Park Square, Milton Park, Abingdon, Oxon OX14 4RN, UK

Bibliomotion is an imprint of the Taylor & Francis Group, an informa business

Library of Congress Cataloging-in-Publication Data

Raskino, Mark, author.
   Digital to the core : remastering leadership for your industry, your enterprise, and yourself / Mark
Raskino and Graham Waller.
      pages cm
   ISBN 978-1-62956-073-1 (hardback) — ISBN 978-1-62956-074-8 (ebook) — ISBN 978-1-62956-075-5
(enhanced ebook)
   1. Information technology—Management.   2. Technological innovations—Management.   3. Leadership.
I. Waller, Graham, author.   II. Title.
   HD30.2.R37 2015
   658'.05—dc23
                                        2015026965

ISBN 978-1-62956-073-1 (hbk)

Printed in Canada

From Mark
To Pauline, Ben, and Danny

From Graham
Thanks to those closest to my core—Alex,
Daniel, Jackie, John, Louise, Patty, and Sheila—
you humble and inspire me every day

CONTENTS

1

Go Digital or Go Home

Rafael Nadal, looking relaxed in sweatpants and a baseball cap, strode up to the net on a tennis court at the Babolat headquarters in Lyon, France. As Nadal played the first few strokes, Eric Babolat, CEO of the French tennis equipment company, watched with nervous anticipation. In April 2012, Babolat had invited Nadal to test the revolutionary new "Connect" racquet, which digitally captures a player's forehands, backhands, smashes, and serves—and sends that data directly to a smartphone or tablet. Richly colored charts told Nadal how much topspin he put on each stroke and whether he hit the ball with the racquet's sweet spot.

"It was like a kid seeing a toy for the first time," Eric Babolat recounted. "You could see it in his eyes," Babolat said of Nadal. "He's a professional player, he has played every day of his life. For the first time he was seeing new images—the data of his game. Before there was tennis without data, now there is tennis with data. It's not a new page in the book. It's a new book."[1]

Babolat's Play racquet contains accelerometer and gyroscope sensors, a digital microprocessor, Bluetooth wireless communications, and a battery. All of these components weigh just fifteen grams and fit inside the handle. A player picking up the conventional version of the same racquet cannot tell the difference; they feel exactly the same.

What's more, the technology isn't available only to Grand Slam professional players. Anyone can buy the racquet for $300 to $400.

This is digital to the core—radical new technology flowing into a company and penetrating right to the core of its product—the racquet—and to the player and the game. The game of tennis can trace its roots back to twelfth-century France. So perhaps it will surprise you to know that until 2013, this revered sport—played, loved, and watched by many millions of people the world over—was defined with only thirty rules. One year after Nadal picked up the Play racquet, in July 2013, Eric Babolat sat in a hotel near the Arc de Triomphe in Paris waiting for a crucial decision from the International Tennis Federation (ITF) Annual General Meeting. "It's like the United Nations," he recalled. "You have people from everywhere, with all languages. They vote for a lot of resolutions."[2] Would they vote for the one he proposed? In a unanimous decision, the ITF approved the thirty-first rule of tennis, which allows the use of Babolat's new racquet *during match play*. Here is the crucial phrase in the new rule: "Player analysis technology may record and/or store information during a match. Such information may only be accessed by a player in accordance with Rule 30."[3]

Babolat's digital innovation helped to literally change the rules of the game. The rule change was crucial to the company's future, because tennis is big business. The size of the tennis industry is $5.55 billion a year in the United States alone,[4] and it is part of a wider global sporting goods industry estimated by some analysts to be over $300 billion.[5]

Taking Digital to the Core for Every Business

A quick sketch of Babolat's history will help you see why this type of digital disruption isn't reserved for greenfield start-ups alone. Every business, no matter how old, has the opportunity and the ability to digitally remaster its products and services. Babolat's story showcases a long history of innovation.

In 1998, Eric Babolat became the fifth-generation leader to run the family-owned company, and he was determined to build on its historic foundation. Today, the company provides both racquets and strings to millions of players all over the world, including top professionals. It was Babolat's great-grandfather, Pierre, who first invented some of the strings the company continues to make. In 1875, a racquet maker asked Pierre to try to make strings from animal gut, using the same process he had already mastered for violin strings. The results were revolutionary. Even today, natural gut strings compare favorably to nylon, polyester, Kevlar, and other modern materials.[6] That invention led the Babolat company eventually to focus wholly on sports racquets. More than a century later, building on that legacy of technological innovation, Eric Babolat is full of passion and pride when he speaks about the world's first and most advanced digital tennis racquet.

He sits in the same 1870s buildings that his great-grandfather used, nondescript and easily missed on the quiet Lyon side street, marked only by a small plaque that guides you to the right doorway. Once you're inside, however, the lobby tells you about the revolution going on—video screens show the connected racquet in action and data projectors paint slogans with light onto the tables: "Innovation," "No Guts, No Glory," "No Limits." It's all about a piece of sports equipment that senses every strike of the ball, calculates and interprets what's happening, and wirelessly sends that information to the player's smartphone or tablet for later analysis.

This individual product revolution is both fascinating and impressive, and we will return to it throughout this book. But it's just one story of how products and services—including yours—will be digitally remastered over the next few years. We wrote this book for CEOs, CIOs, CDOs, strategy officers, and other executives—as we will see in chapter 5, the entire C-level leadership team must be involved. Over the past several years, we have surveyed thousands of CIOs and CEOs to understand their priorities and concerns, and we've worked with CIOs in companies and governments around the globe in their pursuit of digital business. We realized that executives from businesses outside the tech industry need to better comprehend the profound digital disruption now taking place—with more changes on the horizon—and understand how to take action. Often, they are unsure of where to start or how to stay oriented as change builds upon change.

To delve into the secrets of today's successful digital leaders, we supplemented Gartner's vast research base and annual executive survey data with more than thirty interviews of CIOs, CEOs, chief digital and data officers, and other C-level executives from a range of global organizations including Babolat, GE, Ford, Quicken Loans, Publicis, the U.K. government, Tory Burch, BBVA, India's Bharatiya Janata Party, Tokio Marine Insurance, Seoul National University Bundang Hospital, and more. *Digital to the Core* is the result of this research and our many conversations with CIOs in the Gartner community, and it explores how three disruptive digital forces will require you to remaster leadership of your industry, your enterprise, and yourself.

Before we describe these three forces, let's set some context by describing the power and potential of digital business.

What's Different About Digital Business?

Do you assume that everyone is already "doing digital"? If so, then consider that many businesspeople today have a fuzzy view of what digital business is, what the progress stages look like, and how big the gap between companies is. In fact, it's quite alarming how far behind some companies really are. In the 2014 Gartner CEO and Senior Executive Survey, we asked CEOs to answer the following question in their own words: "What does digital business mean in the context of your company and industry?" The responses varied widely, and we found that some companies are far ahead of others.

Industry differences did not explain the wide range of responses. Some responses toward the bottom left of Figure 1.1 were both general and vague. These represent the business leaders whose thinking reflected the attitudes of the 1990s. Those around the center of the chart raised thoughts that were really about the e-business of the early 2000s. Only a small proportion—perhaps 10 percent to 15 percent— expressed specifically directed, newer ideas, such as mobile commerce, the Internet of Things, virtual business, and digital products. Why does it matter if CEOs are a bit vague and fuzzy about digital? The

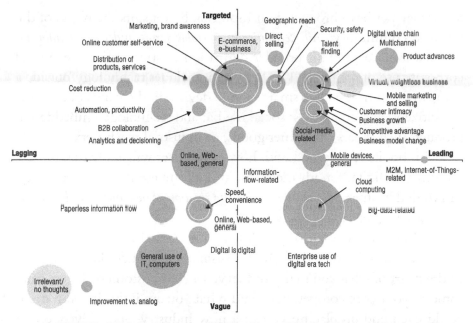

FIGURE 1.1 CEO Responses: "What Does Digital Business Mean for Your Company and industry?"[7]

simple answer is that they will rely on digital business to make their numbers. Gartner's 2015 survey found that CEOs expect that revenues attributable to digital products, marketing, and sales will double from an average of 21 percent in 2014 to 42 percent in 2017.[8] It will be hard for CEOs to lead such growth if they don't understand digital clearly.

As a leader today, you face the difficulty of making the critical decisions that will determine whether the enterprise you lead wins big or ultimately fails. The purpose of this book is to clarify the existing digital business race and orient you to the journey ahead. We also provide a leadership framework to help you *continue* to lead with clarity, even as a whole new set of deeply disruptive technologies and business model changes pile up on the ones already in play.

Let's deal first with the definition problem. What is digital? The simplest technical definition is: *Signal transmission that conveys information through a series of coded pulses representing 1s and 0s (binary code).*[9]

But that's not what most businesspeople mean when they use the term. Gartner has a broader definition that better suits the needs of the business community: *All electronically tractable forms and uses of information and technology.*[10] This broader definition contrasts with the typical corporate use of the term "IT" because it includes technology outside a company's control, such as smart mobile devices in the hands of customers, citizens, and employees; social media; and technology embedded in products such as cars, consumer goods, or industrial machinery.

This book is concerned with how enterprises will apply that understanding of digital for advancement and advantage in an endeavor we call digital business: *digital business is the creation of new business designs by blurring the digital and physical worlds.*[11]

You are probably already familiar with digital marketing because you experience it every day. Digital *business* goes much deeper. It goes to the heart of what you make and serve to your customers. It redefines some of your core competencies and what you are in business to do. It could even end up placing you in a new industry—possibly one that never existed before.

When we say "new business designs," we are referring to new kinds of products and services, business models, and industry models, as well as new ways of creating value for customers. "Blurring the digital and physical" means ending the traditionally clear boundary between the tangible world we live in and the virtual informational world, or "cyberspace," typically thought of as existing inside computers. Perhaps we shouldn't use "digital" in the definition because it's a bit circular, but the word feels comfortable to people in a way that *cyber* and *virtual* don't. Perhaps examples explain digital business best.

Babolat blurs the real-world game of tennis—where yellow felt-covered balls hit racquet strings—with the digital world by measuring millions of tiny movements and vibrations in the racquet head. This data moves though algorithms that analyze and compute the physical movements of the player as they happen. The amount of topspin a player puts on the ball is felt by his arm and measured by the racquet at the same time.

In this book you will find many other examples of organizations and their achievements at the forefront of digital business, including:

- Bharatiya Janata Party (BJP), India's largest political party, which used holograms to project a virtual version of its leader at real-world election rallies and crowdsourced its manifesto
- Ford, which is betting big on connected cars, new forms of mobility innovation, and, one day, autonomous vehicles
- Zappos, a retailer that believes that someday soon your phone might be able to create a 3D scan of your foot, for a better-fitting shoe
- Seoul National University Bundang Hospital that has managed better outcomes for diabetes patients by remote monitoring of glucometers that the patients use in their own homes
- BBVA (Banco Bilbao Vizcaya Argentaria), which is analyzing location data and historical payment transactions to create a better credit score for specific retail sectors, such as pizza restaurants.
- Tory Burch, a company that has created a successful wearable product by enveloping Fitbit activity sensors in its distinctive fashion accessory designs

In each of these cases, the organization has taken digital to the core of its products and services to deliver a new type of customer value. Whether the advances are derived from exquisitely detailed data analyzed to discover patterns, new sensor enablement, or precision control, the core competencies of the digital era may end up being more important than the competencies of each organization's past.

Let's gain some perspective about the potential value created in this world of digital business. The Internet created layers of progress that have come in stages, each building on the layers before it. First, the web enabled companies to display themselves online, allowing them to have a presence. Then came electronic business—e-commerce and e-service—the stage at which companies started to transact directly with customers online. This brought more economic and service value, and from it arose two new management science terms: B2B and B2C (meaning *business to business* and *business to consumer*, respectively). Next came the phase of digital marketing, propelled by search-engine advertising, social media, and mobile apps. Often, value was created by crowds, sharing, and people-to-people connections, sometimes referred to as C2C (*consumer to consumer*).

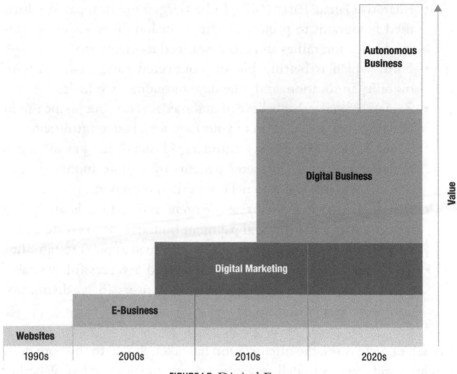

FIGURE I.2 Digital Eras

Now we are in the era of digital business; here, a third entity becomes involved. To the B for business and the C for customer we add T for Things—such as a tennis racquet. This is also referred to as the Internet of Things (IoT). Think about the impact that connected things will have this way: all these new connections considerably expand the universe of possible interactions and ways to create value for customers. We can already glimpse the era that will follow digital business: autonomous business will arrive more quickly than most people expect because technological progress is accelerating rather than advancing at a constant speed. These changes will have profound effects on business.

As the number of digital disruptions to business increases, so does their scale and pace. Consider this: the Kindle 1 e-book reader from Amazon only really became available to U.S. consumers in early 2008.[12] By the end of 2009, e-book sales on Amazon exceeded those

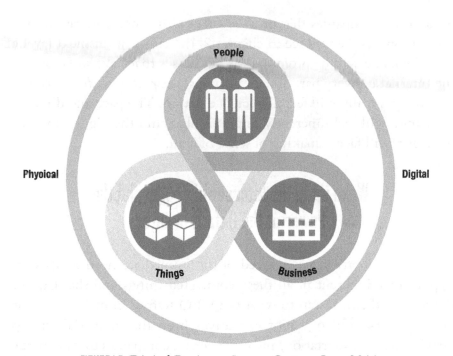

FIGURE 1.3 Digital Business *Source: Gartner, Inc., 2014*

of paper books,[13] and by 2014 the pricing of e-books had become so contentious in the industry that Apple settled a dispute with publishers for $420 million.[14]

This same effect from the world of information goods is now set to impact physical products. The first modern electronic cigarette was invented in China by Hon Lik in 2003.[15] By 2014 global sales were $2.5 billion,[16] and all the major tobacco companies were scrambling to win their slice of the action. By 2023 e-cigarette volumes world-wide are expected to exceed those of "combustible" cigarettes.[17] What will happen to the related industries when your kitchen coffeemaker goes online, your pills become digitally enabled, your shirt senses your respiration rate, and your car comes to collect you from the grocery store automatically? We believe these scenarios could become reality by 2020.

As this Internet of products and their related services emerges, the interactions between them, between us and them, and between them, us, and the companies that provide them will cause innovation upon innovation. As we will see in chapter 2, the effect of this next level of digital change will be profound for businesses that have so far applied the Internet to every part of their business, *except their products*. Some of the changes really will feel like science fiction. The pace and direction of change will feel inherently unpredictable, and the biggest problem managers will face is making of sense of it all.

Wake Up to the Internet of Things and the Power of the Data It Creates

Perhaps you aren't yet convinced of the immediate need to seize the opportunity inherent in all these connected things and the data that flows from them. Listen to what GE CEO Jeffrey Immelt said in late 2014 to a roomful of senior executives from the industrial, energy, health-care, transportation, and engineering companies that are part of an expanding industrial ecosystem that has GE as its hub:

> If you went to bed last night as an industrial company, you are going to wake up in the morning as a software and analytics company. The notion that there's a huge separation between the industrial world and the world of digitalization, analytics, and software—those days are over....It's about transitions and pivots and change; these things never happen in a moment or a day or a month but they sneak up on you and they happen suddenly and there are three changes that we are investing in that are important for our future. The first one's the merger of physics and analytics.... The second big transition is that every customer in the industrial world now knows how to measure and value outcomes.... And the last thing is that it's not just about GE, it's about the extended enterprise.[18]

Immelt was updating the audience on one of the biggest strategic bets in the 120-year history of the firm. On his watch, the company sold its GE Appliances and Lighting consumer appliances division[19] and downsized its GE Capital financial arm.[20] Restructuring is easier than finding new sources of growth, and for growth Immelt's big bet is the "Industrial Internet" strategy GE launched in 2011. The idea came from deep strategic planning work and was based on two key insights: (1) Immelt and his executives saw that software and analytics were being used by GE customers in interesting ways around the operations of their assets. Every customer wanted to get more value and returns out of their assets. (2) GE realized that many companies and their industries were being transformed by the Internet and software. So GE made a bold move, investing $1.0 billion dollars over a three-year period to create GE's Global Software Center, and it brought in Bill Ruh, a veteran software and services engineering leader with senior experience at Cisco and Software AG, to build it. As Ruh, vice president of GE Global Software, put it, "On one side they realized that there was great opportunity and on the other side they had a healthy paranoia that 'if we don't do this, we've got to be careful that we don't get transformed by others who do.' "[21] But what is the "Industrial Internet" that gets Immelt, Ruh, and others at GE so excited?

"In the industrial space especially, we're seeing the number of sensors and their capabilities going up at an exponential rate," Ruh said. "We think of this as the Internet of Things applied to the industrial space. We see the opportunity for enormous productivity and efficiency gains in energy, transportation, aviation, and healthcare through the interconnection of devices enabled via huge amounts of sensors. The key is really analytics on the data, the ability to get deep inside those assets and the processes that surround them and allow people to get more productivity and efficiency out of their assets."[22]

What GE realized is that the data collected by a gas turbine can inform its use, so it burns less fuel to generate more electricity, or the data from a wind turbine can show how the same amount of wind can generate more electricity. "We talk about the power of 1 percent as giving huge gains in these industries. We see this as an opportunity to add $15 trillion to the global GDP over the next fifteen years...with the potential to eliminate enough waste to save the industrial world more than $150 billion annually," Ruh said.[23]

GE's remastering of aero engines and wind turbines is akin to

Babolat's changes to tennis racquets, only on an immense scale. GE wants to compare and optimize all of the world's airplane engines, using the data from the sensors within them—even if one engine can generate a terabyte of data in just one flight. GE's software and sensors can optimize a wind farm by analyzing the airflow over one turbine and adjusting all the others in the array to account for the turbulence. In every case, the one or two percentage points of increased efficiency through data analytics could yield tens of billions of dollars' worth of industrial efficiency savings. Big machines, big operating costs, big money, big strategy. For GE, this is a major change in direction, one that involves creating the kind of computing, data management, software, and analytics capabilities that perhaps only companies like Google and IBM have had in the past.

When data from the third entity—things—gets involved, digital business must contend with the physical world and all its complications: hot and cold, loud and quiet, micro and macro, longstanding and temporary, moving and static, wet and dry. The real world adds a lot of complexity. Here, the number of permutations and combinations of businesses, people, and things becomes very large. Gartner predicts that by 2020 twenty-five billion things will be connected to the Internet[24] and estimates that there are at least 130 million enterprises. There are already three billion people online worldwide.[25] Business times people times things (B x P x T) means that the number of possible interactions and the creative opportunities and unexpected breakthroughs and threats will grow. Explosively.

This fundamental factor leads to an unavoidable truth—the future is becoming just too complex to predict using traditional approaches. You cannot know what you will need to know. You can't calculate and plan sufficient scenarios. Yet you must do *something* because the digital business world will be a turbulent and unforgiving place where winner-take-all outcomes will be common and the disrupters themselves will be disrupted.

Digital business will cause deeper business change than Internet technology created in the past. You will need to take digital right to the core of everything you know and rely on. As a result, you will need to remaster your industry and your enterprise, but to do those things you will also need to remaster yourself—your leadership skills and behaviors—your mind set, and the way you see the digital world.

Master Digital Outside-In

Often, changes to the way you manage a business are under your full control. The digital changes ahead will not be like that. Technology will revolutionize the things people and businesses use in everyday life so much that the very foundation of your industry is likely to be undermined. For this reason, there is no point trying to understand and lead digital change in isolation from within your organization's four walls. There is no chance that you can lead successful digital change by some miracle of introspection that happens to align with markets in flux with the right kind of change at the right time. Without a hard look at the radical changes taking place in the *outside* world first, your attempts at digital change will be incremental and weak.

First, therefore, we will help you examine the change forces that digital progress causes or amplifies and look at how those reshape industries. After that, we will explain what kinds of change these forces will require within your enterprise and how your own leadership style needs to adapt. This approach sets up an outside–in framework of three key forces that impact at three different levels of view, enabling you to remap your industry, remodel your enterprise, and remake yourself.

We will examine each of the intersection points between the forces and the levels following this outside–in progression, chapter by chapter. In part 1 we'll describe the nuances of each disruptive force so that you can fully embrace its impact on your industry and understand how to leverage it for business gain. Part 2 explores how to lead your enterprise in a way that harnesses each disruptive force. For example, we'll look at how compound uncertainties impact at an enterprise level, requiring you to educate a digitally savvy C-suite and board. In part 3, we describe six leadership styles to inspire your journey through digital business.

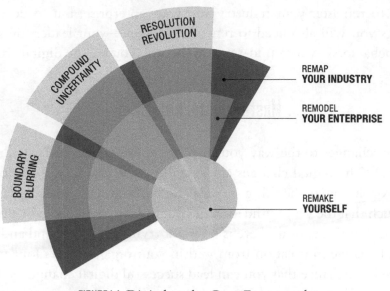

FIGURE 1.4 Digital to the Core Framework

Three Disruptive Digital Forces Drive Remastery

Digital progress sets up winds of change that affect the way business and society operate. The strength and energy of these winds are sufficient to coerce and compel responses from all players in a market—these huge externalities that surround all companies cannot be ignored, so we call them "forces." We believe that you can clarify the uncertainty surrounding digital by focusing on three irrefutable and highly disruptive macro forces.

1. **Resolution revolution:** The effect of being able to see and sense what is happening in both the physical and digital worlds in ever greater fidelity and detail, then understanding and more precisely controlling things, events, and outcomes.

2. **Compound uncertainty:** The combined and complex effects of digital change that undermine and shift the mind-sets, structures, and practices on which leaders have previously relied. The key uncertainties are in three areas: technology, culture, and regulation.

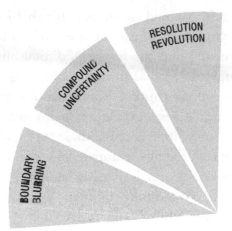

FIGURE 1.5 The Three Disruptive Digital Forces

3. **Boundary blurring:** The merging of digital and physical worlds, leading to alterations in the core products, propositions, and possibilities for industries as we know them and softening the dividing lines between industries. The effect then cascades across ecosystems, enterprises, people, and things.

Our goal is to help you understand and evaluate these forces, then build competencies that exploit their immense power rather than swimming against their riptide. The task, then, is to commit to leading at three different levels: industry, enterprise, and self. Failure to attend to all three forces will lead you to be tossed in the waves of industry disruption and quite possibly be swept away. Failure to lead at all three levels will cause your leadership to be weak and temporary.

Remaster Your Industry, Your Enterprise, and Yourself

Despite the fact that they are very different kinds of companies, GE and Babolat have something in common: both are early movers making a big strategic bet and potentially risking the company reputation on a major shift to digital business. On the other hand, the risk of not making these big moves could be higher. It's this kind of risky but ultimately necessary move that inspired us to write a book to help you lead your own company into the future of digital business. Digital is no longer a backing vocal; it has moved center stage to become part of the main act. We don't think GE and Babolat are unusual; they just launched their initiatives a bit earlier than most. Every company is going to need leaders who help make these types of visionary shifts. Perhaps, in the long run, the new competencies will be commonplace. Today, comprehension of and leadership ability in digital business change are in short supply and thus command a market premium.

The leaders at GE, Babolat, and many of the organizations we interviewed for this book operate at all three levels of the framework for remastering leadership for the digital age.

1. **Remap your industry:** How must your worldview change and what fundamental industry paradigms must you rethink?
2. **Remodel your enterprise:** What does your enterprise need to become and how will you redefine your company?
3. **Remake yourself:** Who do you need to be and how must you remake yourself to thrive as a leader in the digital era?

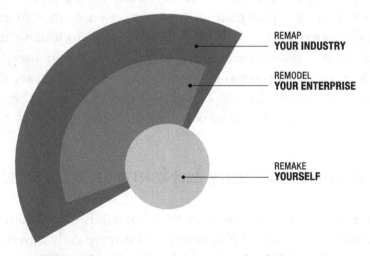

FIGURE 1.6 The Three Leadership Levels of Abstraction

Use the Framework to Take Digital to the Core

You will have to remap your industry, or quickly adjust to a remapped industry, possibly several times, as different actors test and transgress the blurring boundaries. You will need to remodel your enterprise so that it can create and serve the new kinds of value demanded by customers in a digital world. And you will have to remake yourself as a leader, taking on new skills and new personas, and be prepared to engage new kinds of professionals and apply new thinking tools.

Together, the three digital forces and three leadership levels create the framework for taking digital to the core of your business and leadership style.

Read this book from end to end, tackle it in sections that deal with the levels of change, or skip to the chapters that follow a force, its implications, and ways to handle the changes. We hope you will find the framework useful as a device for locating and then dipping into the ideas that will help you solve a specific problem in your digital leadership work.

We chose GE and Babolat as our opening stories after careful

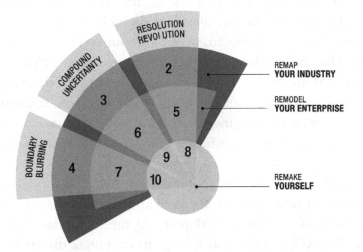

FIGURE 1.7 Digital to the Core Framework—Chapter by Chapter

consideration. One is a massive U.S. public corporation in heavy indus-trial products, while the other is a far smaller, privately held French family firm in a consumer products sector. Both, however, have been in business for more than a century and neither has previously been part of the information technology sector. We hope an understanding of their journeys will help you take digital to the core. While we'll draw on some of the business techniques and hear directly from "born-digital" firms such as Orbitz and Zappos, we recognize that they started in a different greenfield place, so you can't simply copy them. Rather, you will hear new practices from digital leaders in car com-panies, banks, insurers, and government organizations. These are the visionary leaders who will take digital to the core for the 90 percent of the economy that wasn't born that way. They are remastering leader-ship for the digital age.

Digital Business Can Power Your Success

On September 21, 2014, Babolat's revolutionary racquet had its first official international match play victory when Karolína Plíšková won the women's WTA International Korea Open. Rafael Nadal started using the racquet in professional match play in 2015. By the end of 2014, Babolat Play racquets had digitally recorded more than thirty-three million shots, from 97,000 hours of play in 33,000 matches. The racquet has won industry awards and helped Babolat become the number-one brand among international tennis players for technical innovation, ahead of far larger sports equipment mak-ers.[26] Eric Babolat is changing the rules of the game, and we believe him when he says that in the future "tennis without data will not be possible."[27]

If a small, family-owned, centuries-old maker of animal-gut rac-quet strings can take digital to the core and revolutionize its industry, then so can you. If a huge, 120-year-old multinational engineering enterprise like GE can radically change its corporate direction to take digital to the core and revolutionize its industry, then so can you. It's all about your leadership.

Actionable Takeaways

Plan for a whole new level of change—it's called digital business. Digital business takes a giant step from the preceding eras of digital marketing and online e-commerce, blurring the digital and physical worlds and generating data that creates new products and services capable of revolutionizing industries.

Take an outside–in view to get the right perspective. To understand the forces at work and to lead sufficiently deep change, step out of the usual bounding frame to consider industry-level change and disruption from many angles. The change will be deep enough to warrant action at executive-committee level and board level.

Assess the three key forces at work to exploit them to your advantage. The force of *resolution revolution,* enables you to see the world in higher fidelity and then to understand and control that world with greater precision. The force of *compound uncertainty* makes it hard, though not impossible, to know when the technology, culture, and regulation will align to create your moment to pounce. Inaction is risky, because the force of *boundary blurring* enables powerful new, unusual competitors to enter your industry and redefine it.

Address change at three levels to make deep rather than superficial progress. To win in digital business you need to remap your industry, in collaboration with others. To do this, remodel your enterprise, for example by upgrading the C-suite and board to create new competencies. To lead these changes effectively, remake yourself as an explorer, ambassador, educator, clarifier, attractor, and cartographer.

Apply the digital-to-the-core framework to stay oriented. At times, it will feel like everything is changing and there are no anchor points along your digital business journey. The framework in this book was designed specifically to help you find your course as you navigate the complex leadership challenges ahead.

PART I

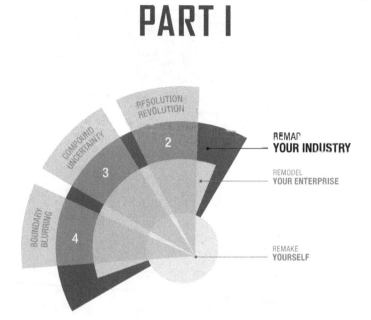

2

Every Product Will Be Digitally Remastered

As digital technologies advance, they sense the world around us in ever finer detail. Tiny sensors become part of products, and the data they generate allows us to see new patterns, distinguish variations, and discover new realities. Connecting things to the Internet allows us to control their operation remotely and manage the everyday scenarios they are part of with far greater precision. Applying these new function and service possibilities to existing products enables us to create far superior digital versions. Using this approach, we can remaster and upgrade any product. New business models based on these enhanced capabilities will emerge, and the companies that apply them will become the new masters of their industries.

At the 2015 Consumer Electronics Show (CES) in Las Vegas, 170,000 professionals walked 2.2 million square feet of show floor to get a first look at the cool gadgets and new digital technology ideas of 34,000 exhibiting companies. Expectations were sky high as attendees waited for exciting new announcements and technological breakthroughs. Mark Fields, CEO of Ford, did not disappoint. He told the audience that autonomous cars are the real deal and that eventually Ford intends to make them available to the masses, just as Henry Ford did with the automobile. Fields also announced Ford Smart Mobility, describing it as "our plan to use innovation to take Ford to the next level in connectivity, in mobility, in autonomous vehicles, the customer experience, and big data. And a first critical step is the creation of twenty-five mobility experiments across the globe, all designed to help us change the way the world moves."[1]

In an e-mail interview for this book, Fields elaborated on the depth and significance of the market changes facing Ford today:

> Without question, we are embarking on one of the most transformative periods in the history of Ford. The world is changing. People interact in new ways. They gather and share information differently and consume products and services in more ways than we have ever seen before.
>
> We understand that the winners will be the innovators, the disrupters, and those willing to break with tradition and find new answers. So we are pushing ourselves even harder to think, to act, and to disrupt like a start-up, anticipating customers' wants and needs ten years down the road.[2]

In the early twentieth century, Henry Ford used steel to revolutionize mass production. In the early twenty-first century, Mark Fields uses digital and the resolution revolution to remaster Ford, taking it from a carmaker to a company focused on mobility. "We're driving to be both a product and a mobility company," Fields declared at CES, "and ultimately change the way the world moves." How the world moves is precisely what Fields and Ford seek to remaster. Henry Ford created a car that every person could drive. Mark Fields plans to create a car that every person can ride.[3] As vehicles become more autonomous, we will look to them more as a service than as a product.

Fields told us:

> On autonomous vehicles, Ford already is a leader, with semi-autonomous vehicles on the road today that use software and sensors to steer into both parallel and perpendicular parking spaces, adjust speed in traffic, or apply the brakes in an

emergency. We also have fully autonomous research vehicles on the road, too, and are committed to making autonomous vehicle technology widely accessible—and not just for premium buyers. At the same time, we are rethinking the vehicle ownership experience for future customers. This includes studying new plans for fractional ownership for those who do not want or need full-time access to a vehicle.[4]

A Revolution in the Resolution of Things

An autonomous car's ability to drive itself safely relies on what it can *see*. Ford's experimental vehicle uses four LIDAR sensors to generate a real-time, three-dimensional map of the vehicle's surrounding environment. "Full automation will be possible in areas where high-definition mapping is possible, along with favorable environmental conditions for the vehicle's sensors," said Ford's CTO of product development, Raj Nair.[5] Technology's ability to sense, capture, and process entirely new kinds of data in ever richer detail leads to the big breakthroughs that underpin the digital business age. We call this fundamental dimension of progress the resolution revolution.

But this increasing fidelity is not limited to cars and it's not limited to seeing. GE's transition to the industrial Internet stems from this same resolution revolution. "Almost every industrial product, certainly all the industrial products that we manufacture today, have sensors on them and have the ability to take real-time continuous data streams as they're being used," GE's CEO Jeffrey Immelt said. "So big rotating

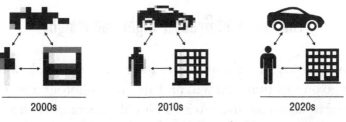

| 2000s | 2010s | 2020s |

FIGURE 2.1 Resolution Revolution

equipment, jet engines, gas turbines, MRI scanners, locomotives now are able to take big continuous streams of data and pervasive data going forward in the future."[6]

The impact of the resolution revolution extends beyond large engineering companies. Smartphones contain at least a dozen powerful environmental sensors, including ones that detect light, sound, acceleration, gravity, rotation, location, temperature, humidity, electromagnetic field strength, biometric data, and more. This data can be monitored and used by any mobile app developer to help users measure sound levels, score their driving safety,[7] or even turn the phone into a kind of weather station.[8]

Whether the change involves consumer products like cars and tennis racquets or services like usage-based insurance, whether it takes place in America or in Asia, and whether it's occurring at Fortune 500 public companies or small family-run firms, the same big shift is underway. The technology of the digital information age is penetrating *right inside* the things companies make, sensing how the things operate, and recording their environment and use in incredible detail. We have never had data like this before: we can measure and inspect every rotation of a fan blade and every forehand shot played.

We're experiencing a revolution in the resolution of the information at our disposal, and it's bringing a new level of clarity to what we can see about our customers, our operations, our competitors, and, indeed, the world around us. This revolution will power dramatic breakthroughs, remastery, and improvements in everything we do. Leaders who underestimate the power of this transformative force risk failure.

The Power of Greater Sight and Insight

Here's another way of thinking about the resolution revolution. When you next go on vacation, you will probably take photographs. However you choose to take a picture—with a digital camera or with a phone—there is a single word you will use to describe the image quality the device offers: "megapixel." Mexapixel is an example of a technology word that has become everyday language for us all. It's a measure of detail and definition. It's shorthand used to describe how much clarity you will get, how much you can see, how far you can zoom in. This resolution has brought all kinds of secondary benefits and uses. For example, you can crop to get a good-quality picture of a single person from a group shot. Services exist that convert your pictures to a screen saver for your big flat-screen TV, because the pictures are now good enough to be blown up to a large size. An app called Scoopshot will help you get paid for images media outlets use in a story, because your phone camera now has nearly professional-grade resolution.

Megapixels describe the number of individual elements, arrayed on the sensor inside the camera, upon which the light falls when the shutter is opened. Because the sensor is a silicon-based microprocessor, its capability has advanced at the pace of Moore's law (the tendency of computing power to double every two years[9]). Cameras offer more megapixels at lower cost today than they did a few years ago. In fact, the rate of progress has been exponential. That force of exponential improvement in the detail with which we can see or measure our world is not unique to cameras: it applies to many items and will soon extend into everything. Yes, *everything*. Take, for example, cigarettes.

Anything Can Be Digitalized

In 2012 one of the big three U.S. tobacco companies, Lorillard, acquired an electronic cigarette maker called Blu. At the time, Lorillard CEO Murray Kessler said, "The performance of [e-cigarettes] over the next few years will be like the digital camera or anything else—it will get better and better, more and more affordable, and that's when you'll really see the category take off."[10] Lorillard was fairly early to the e-cigarette game among big tobacco companies, and Kessler was smart enough to foresee the nonlinear progress rate of this fundamentally digital technology. Essentially, a tiny microprocessor inside the electronic cigarette controls the generation of flavor and nicotine-infused steam for the user to inhale, and that machine creates and manipulates data.

It didn't take long for Reynolds American, maker of the Vuse e-cigarette, to market the technology as "digital," saying that its product "contains a Vapor Delivery Processor that uses algorithms in the same way a computer does, therefore we refer to it as 'digital'....The Vapor Delivery Processor works with the SmartMemory to monitor and adjust the power and heat delivered to the cartridge up to 2,000 times a second."[11]

These fine-grained sensing and controlling actions represent a radical shift in an industry that traditionally distributed leaf-based products in bulk consignments via wholesalers and distributors. The manufacturers didn't have information about their end-user customers. Looking forward, within the space of only a few years e-cigarette manufacturers may be able to discover in microscopic detail how their customers consume a digitalized substitute product, puff by puff, moment by moment, location by location, flavor by flavor. This is the revolution in resolution that allows businesses to see into their markets and precisely control products as they are used.

Future "tobacco" companies might operate Internet-based, direct-sell, razor-blade business models for supplying e-cigarette nicotine juice as a service. They will know in incredible detail which flavors are in fashion—bubblegum, aniseed, pineapple, or cappuccino (yes, these are real examples). They will eventually know time-of-day trends and whether the product is consumed when the user is alone or in social situations, with location pinned down to city or block level, if needed. They will know their consumers not via surveys and focus groups but directly from the data coming out of the sensors that control the "vaping" their users are doing every day. One company has already registered a patent for e-cigarette connection and data collection.[12] One day we might even see a "pay per puff" business model.

Every Product and Service Will Be Digitally Remastered

Eventually, the resolution revolution will take over every product in every industry. The data being gathered within the products, and the precision of control that can be exercised over their use and monetization, will become ever more detailed. There are no limits to this force: it applies to B2B and B2C companies; it applies to products of all sizes, from large fields of wind turbines to cars, coffee machines, cigarettes, batteries, and even individual pills. The miniaturization effects of Moore's law apply as products provide more and more detailed resolution and businesses gain finer-grained control from smaller sensors and actuators at the same time.

At the extreme, these products include Internet-connected sensors small enough for a human being to ingest and excrete. Proteus Digital Health, for example, has developed sensor-enabled medication that can monitor the time a pill is taken. A tiny sensor the size of a grain of sand can be embedded in any pill—the sensor is made of everyday metals that are safe to consume. When it contacts stomach acid, a small charge is generated that powers the circuit. The sensor sends a unique ID number wirelessly to a body-worn disposable patch that relays it by Bluetooth to a smartphone.[13] By digitally remastering a pill in this way, new sources of value and service can be enabled. For example, doctors or family members can track patients to make sure that the right patient takes the right pill at the right time. Or the sensor can alert a caregiver that a patient or loved one has not ingested critical medication. We did say *anything* can be made digital.

In every area that companies want to deliver and manage products or services more effectively for customers, the resolution of the information available to assist them will become more and more detailed. Every time such an increase in resolution happens, the game will change. The examples in Table 2.2 illustrate of some of the possibilities, but the same principles of higher fidelity and more precise control apply everywhere.

Trump or Be Trumped

The increase in resolution detail and precision control that can be applied and mastered is not a one-time step—it's a repeating cycle. For example, in the oil industry there is a race to gain more and more detail and resolution in an area the oil supermajors often call the "digital oil field." In 2013, Dana Deasy, then CIO of BP, told us to imagine exploring for oil in the middle of the Gulf of Oman desert using a

	Yesterday	Today	Tomorrow	One Day
Medicine	Prescribed	Dispensed	Accessed	Consumed
Tennis Play	Service speed	Line calls	Topspin	Player mind-set
Cigarette Consumption	Consignment	Packet	Use	Puff
Car Driving	Mileage	Car location	Door use	Driver mood
Weather Forecasting	Area	District	Farm	Field
News Readership	Demographic	Subscriber	Article	Phrase
Electricity Use	Substation	Home	Device	Activity
Health	Age and gender	Lifestyle	Activities	Biometrics
Criminal DNA Profile	Weeks	Hours	Minutes	Seconds
Personal Payment	3 days	3 minutes	30 seconds	3 seconds
Brand Management	Recall	Net promoter	Social sentiment	Neural response

TABLE 2.2 Examples of Resolution Revolution Progress

huge machine that vibrates the earth and captures the echo data for analysis. The next step is to take that data and generate a 3D image from it, so that geologists can see what is happening underground and do a seismic assessment. Back in 2010, visualizing an underground area the size of a large concert hall would have taken four to five months of computer processing time. But by 2013, Deasy said, "We are doing that in four to five hours. And in the next four to five years, we'll be doing that in four to five minutes."[14]

In the oil industry, the ability to take huge amounts of detailed sensor data from the field, send it over the Internet, then crunch it inside high-power, memory-based computing facilities will change the game again and again. This capability powers critical commercial competencies such as "time to first oil" in exploration.

Arjen Dorland, EVP of technical and competitive IT at Royal Dutch Shell, acknowledged the value of these capabilities in helping the company stay competitive. "One of our aims in this space is summarized in a catch phrase, 'See what others can't see,'" explained Dorland. "By using image interpretation, big data handling, and then modeling and optimization review, we hope to find oil and gas resources that were missed or which others were not able to spot."[15]

For Shell this isn't just a tactical capability, it is deeply strategic. According to Dorland, it's the heart of Shell's business and future. The reserves replacement is one of the key characteristics of a major oil and gas company, and it is driven by technology. It's not uncommon for an offshore exploration well to cost on the order of $200 million. "It's a lot cheaper to drill a well in simulation, in a computer environment, than to drill it in reality," Dorland said. "If we invest in better visualization, better big data handling, better modeling, and reduce the failure risk of drilling those expensive wells only by a couple of percentage points, that is actually very good business."

Precision Response and Control Are the Key to Value

Over the last twenty years or so, car-tracking "telematics" services have gradually been evolved by provider services such as GM's OnStar. However, most of the focus has traditionally been on emergencies such as accidents and theft. Soon, these services will undergo a resolution revolution.

Instead of tracking a car, imagine tracking every part of the car. Instead of being able to remotely control one big part like the engine, imagine being able to control everything—the fuel filler cap, the trunk, the heater. Now imagine being able to control those parts as part of everyday service rather than on an occasional emergency basis. Instead of the service being available via a special call center to select customers, imagine it being available to anyone.

That's how Klas Bendrik, CIO of Volvo Cars, plans to take advantage of the continuing revolution in resolution and precision control. Volvo On Call and Sensus Connect services now come with every car the company makes.[16] The automaker has been market testing a new service that lets organizations and individuals directly access Volvo car doors via a one-time-use digital key sent to a person's smartphone. The digital key will open one door on one car for a specified period of time.

Once used, it expires. For example, a driver could ask a work colleague to retrieve something she forgot in her car by sending a temporary digital key to the colleague's phone. Or a driver could make a key available to a commercial service. Bendrik explained: "For instance, you can have food or other goods delivered directly to the trunk of your car. An e-commerce delivery driver locates your car and opens your trunk through a smartphone or tablet app. You can follow the process on your own phone or tablet, to see when your car is opened, accessed, and locked again—in real time. Once it is done, the car is locked and the one-time digital key will cease to exist."

McDonald's has already experimented with the opportunity to influence hundreds of millions of customers as they consume its products. McDonald's 2014 World Cup promotion leveraged more than a billion French fry boxes, connecting that real-world packaging to a mobile-enabled virtual experience. To play, customers downloaded the free app onto their smartphones or tablets. They then aimed their device's camera at the football-themed fry box. The mobile device screen showed the real-world view of a box of fries sitting on a table, with overlaid graphics that made it look like a soccer game. The restaurant table was the field and the fry box was the goal. The player had to try to flick a virtual ball, displayed on the screen, into the goal. People could play a game with various levels of difficulty, then share their trick shots over social media. Interactions between consumers' mobile phones, social media, and the physical food packaging made this possible, a classic case of the boundary blurring between the digital and physical worlds that is a hallmark of digital business.[17]

Every Industry Will Be Remastered

Thus far, a small number of industries have been deeply disrupted and fundamentally redefined as a result of digitalization. Examples include music, newspapers, travel agencies, books, and photographic film. In each case, customer needs are now being served in completely new ways, like downloading and streaming music or reading e-books instead of printed books. Many people have assumed that such deep digitalization impacts will be limited to a small subset of "bit industries," where the underlying product is fundamentally information. The "atom" industries—in which the product or service is fundamentally a feature of the physical world, such as transporting people in cars—have been thought to be less vulnerable.[18] Some information industries that computerized decades ago, such as insurance and banking, believed they were already substantially digital. The situation has changed, and so must those mind-sets, fundamental beliefs, and assumptions.

Digital remastery of an industry takes place, in parallel, at two levels:

1. A change of the firms that dictate the industry direction—the masters
2. An upgrading or reinvention of the product or service itself via new core competencies

Deep digital change causes a shift in the center of value creation. Value creation is the activity that increases the worth of products or services for customers. For example, in local small business advertising, over the past ten to fifteen years, the center of gravity in value creation shifted from ads placed in printed paper phone directories and local newspapers to ad words in Internet search engines and banner ads on websites.

Payments system companies such as Visa understand the opportunities and risks inherent in this shift. "The industry has moved to a changing technology that has liberated consumers to transact anytime, pay anybody, buy anything, anytime, anyplace, anywhere on any device," said Steve Perry, chief digital officer at Visa Europe. "What that means is the liberation of the individual. It means that new entrants can come in and provide instant gratification of account balances, balance transfers, loyalty rewards, and payments. For the first time in economic history, the fulfillment of consumer needs and wants is becoming instantaneous."[19] We will explore Visa's story in more depth in chapter 5.

The competencies (combinations of skills, techniques, and assets) required to deliver the newer kind of value creation are not the same as those needed to achieve the old. Major incumbent firms in an industry must gradually let go of the old and adopt the new. If the incumbents are slow or are incapable of making the shift to the new capability, then a new entrant will inevitably develop it. Eventually, the masters of the new methods of value creation will become the masters of the redefined industry. Every industry will be remastered, whether the incumbents do it, the new entrants do it, or the battle between them does it.

There is a second, parallel meaning of *remastery*. In the field of audio and video, since the early 1960s, the term "remaster" has been used to describe the process of creating a new master recording of higher quality. For example, the original *Star Trek* TV programs made in 1964 can be watched today in high definition, with 5.1 surround sound, on a large flat-screen TV far better than they could have been seen by anyone, even the director himself, when first broadcast. This digital reimagining and re-rendering of products is the other level of remastery at work.

It's not just audio and visual media that can be remastered, however; potentially any product can be. This idea is part literal, part analogy. A bank account that existed in 1964 with the same account number can be digitally revolutionized directly into smartphone form. An individual cigarette from 1964 cannot be directly remade—but that "Mad Men cool" vibe can be re-rendered and reimagined for a twenty-first-century setting in the form of a digitally controlled e-cigarette. Multiple product-transforming technologies that once existed only in the realm of sci-fi—such as AI, robotics, and 3D printing—are now reality.

The challenge ahead for business leaders is to stay in control as both their industry and its products are digitally remastered not once but multiple times. Trump or be trumped. This will be an exciting opportunity, but also extremely testing.

Digital Penetrates to the Core

Over the past twenty years, packaged business applications software and Internet enablement have transformed nearly every aspect of the way a corporation operates on a daily basis, or so it seems. Figure 2.3 illustrates what has happened.

FIGURE 2.3 Internet-Era Technologies Have Often Changed Every Aspect of the Enterprise, Except the Core Product Itself

On the sell side of the business, digital media have elevated marketing communications, CRM has empowered customer interaction, and e-commerce has helped automate and advance selling. On the supply side, electronic procurement and supply chain management have helped improve buying efficiency, reduce inventory, drive just-in-time methods, and assure traceability. On the stakeholder side, we have blogs, tweets, online videos, image libraries, and electronic press releases all helping management to engage with the news media and other interested parties. Our companies have great investor websites for stockholders and recruitment websites to attract talent.

Inside the company we have integrated, advanced ERP systems to help manage processes and operations, together with business intelligence (BI) systems to keep management apprised and in control of all that activity. Our knowledge workers collaborate more effectively using e-mail, messaging, screen sharing, video conferencing, and many other tools. So, it seems technology has penetrated everything, everywhere across the company. But there is one last area that has often remained dark and untouched—the product or service itself.

Over the past twenty years of IT advancement, most businesses have changed everything *but* the product. Even if they now possess advanced, Internet-enabled business models, they are actually making and selling pretty much the same kind of products they were making in 1994. Changing the product is the final step, and the biggest shock of all. Internet-connected and embedded digital functions will become a key part of your product and the value your customer buys. This value may represent 20 percent, 40 percent, or 60 percent of what the customer acknowledges and pays for.

This customer value is easily explained using cars as an example that everyone can see and understand. When it comes to automobiles, the percentage of customer-perceived and derived value that is digital (rather than painted body panels, leather upholstery, and metal combustion engine) continues to increase. Young people may be as likely to buy a car for its Bluetooth media integration and voice recognition as its fuel efficiency. Some of the advertisements on television reflect this trend. Tomorrow's ads will promote the self-driving feature or the heads-up display with built-in driving scene hazard recognition and analysis.

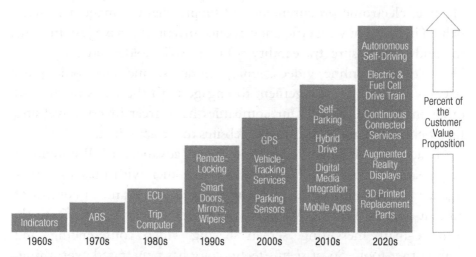

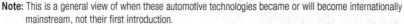
Note: This is a general view of when these automotive technologies became or will become internationally mainstream, not their first introduction.

FIGURE 2.4 Evolution of the Auto Industry

Making and selling computers, software, telecommunications, or data services will remain the job of the IT industry. However, most industries will embed computing, software functionality, communication, and data services into the products they make and sell. When that happens, capabilities in those areas, specialized to each industry domain, will become a part of the differentiating core competency. In that sense, every company will need to become a technology company—at least in part.

We recognize that this idea may be challenging, and perhaps you cannot yet see why your company might need to become more tech centric. Failure to understand this need could represent a dangerous blind spot. See chapter 4 for a deeper explanation.

Products and Services Will Be Transformed

Try this exercise: first, think of any activity you engage in, in your everyday home, family, or leisure life. Second, think of any physical object you associate with that activity. We are confident that the random object in your mind can be transformed by digital technologies to provide far greater utility. Any object can be partly digitalized.

During 2013 and 2014, we tested this idea at CIO workshop sessions held at Gartner conferences in Japan, the United States, and Europe. Teams of CIOs quickly and easily came up with serious value-adding functions for a range of objects they used, including a golf club, axe, diving mask, garden hoe, sausage, and dog collar. All the brainstorming sessions yielded lists of plausible features—often based on the kinds of technologies we find today embedded in advanced smartphones.

Physical products today can be significantly enhanced by adding combinations of the following digital elements:

- Sensors
- Displays and indicators
- Actuators and manipulators
- Microcontrollers
- Onboard analytics

- Memory
- Wireless-connected services
- Remote controls

This rich array of innovation capabilities has already begun to transform many everyday products and some industrial ones. The following examples are all available today:

- E-cigarette—heats liquid into a nicotine-laced vapor instead of burning tobacco
- Digital billboard—senses who is viewing and responds to that person
- Smart soccer ball—reports its speed, direction, and other data to a mobile device
- Augmented-reality ski goggles—show a radar-like display of skiers' locations
- Car smartphone remote control—provides access to the air conditioning controls or fuel gauge
- Robot golf course lawnmower—repeats perfect pattern cutting of greens
- Crypto currencies—substitute for conventional government-issued money
- Smart-home lightbulbs—set precise color hue and brightness remotely

In many industries, fundamental revolutions in features, functions, and performance are occurring. In some cases, products that have been relegated to commodity status for decades are now being differentiated. In other cases, the digitalization of products and services takes them outside the bounds of conventional regulatory control, at least in the short term.

Imagine a world full of active, connected digital products. The status messages and sensor readings from these products will stream wirelessly to a local point such as a smartphone or Wi-Fi router. The data will continue from there to the cloud. This data will paint a rich, live picture of activities going on in business and in personal lives, and it

will create many "business moments" of opportunity to provide services. The existence of the data means that there is an opportunity
for information asymmetry—and, therefore, competitive advantage
within service industries.

For example, life insurers can know the exact moments of fear
in our lives, and when we might think about buying insurance, for
example when we stare down a difficult slope while off-piste skiing
or screech to halt suddenly on a highway. They don't need to spend
money on ads to remind us to worry.

Coffee machines can know when a homeowner is running out of
capsules and automatically reorder. Cars can know when a driver
feels stressed—and download appropriate soothing ambient or classical
music. Or they can know when a driver is overly fatigued and provide
visual and sound stimuli. For financial payments and services companies, these digitally enhanced products might one day become semi-
autonomous agents, authorized to buy things on their owner's behalf.

When many vehicles start to drive themselves, the radar-like maps
of roads they must navigate will create a constantly updating, detailed
3D picture of the streetscape. Government agencies and services firms
might use this data to spot small changes—such as dumped trash or
traffic signals knocked out of alignment.

Investment fund managers who find government economic data
too infrequent or questionable and financial reporting data inad-
equate will have many other places to hunt. Aggregated data about
electricity consumption, driving activity, truck routes, human weight
fluctuations, and many other sources could inform them about how
economies and industries are really performing.

Simply put, those enterprises that find ways to access the combined
data will be able to understand customer needs earlier, and to serve
them more precisely, than those that continue to fly blind.

New Core Competencies

The term "core competency" has been central to business strategy
thinking ever since it was first proposed by Gary Hamel and C.K.

Prahalad in "The Core Competence of the Corporation" in 1990. The concept, however, is often diluted and misused. In its original form, the authors pointed to core competencies as capabilities that uniquely differentiated a business—not just things that are important. For example, many companies have CRM as a strong capability, but that does not make it a core competency. In their original work, Hamel and Prahalad cited as an example of a core competency engine design at Honda, which used the competency to build motorcycles, lawnmowers, and boat engines.

The e-business era, as we discussed in chapter 1, resulted in changes to nearly every operating part of a business except the core competency. Insurers still operated based on conventional underwriting, retail banks competed on branding and rate differences, and consumer packaged goods companies still competed on plastic packaging shape and color. Methods of marketing and selling changed, but core products did not; thus, true core competencies remained substantially the same.

What will an engine maker do in a world of digitally controlled electric cars? What will an insurer do in a world where open-data-informed AI systems can outsmart underwriters? What will a food manufacturer do in a world where nutrition-tracking RFID tags are ingestible and packaging can interact with the Internet? What will a bank do in a world of crypto currencies and peer-to-peer social lending?

A company's core foundation can be changed—even what it understands itself to be, and what industry it thinks it is in. For example, if a retailer 3D prints a product on demand from a CAD design it just negotiated for in a bot-controlled auction, is it a design house, a manufacturer, or a retailer? If a cleaning services company switches from using people to using robots, does it suddenly become part of a capital-intensive industry?

In the last few pages we introduced disruptive ideas and examples. Your head might be spinning with an overload of all the possibilities and change dimensions in play, leaving you frozen and directionless. That happens to us, too, quite regularly. The best way to cope is to elevate and simplify your view.

Your industry will be changed by the following digital progress:

1. Connected sensors and the data they generate will allow you to see and inspect your world in finer detail and higher fidelity; this is the **revolution in resolution**.
2. Your ability to remotely update or manipulate individual things and elements in your world, with great exactitude, is also improving; this is **precision response and control**.

The resolution revolution and precision response and control are advancing in repeating cycles at the pace of Moore's law. They are accelerating. Such acceleration will trip up many business thinkers who have been used to pedestrian and linear progress rates in their products, services, and business models. Disruptive innovation is open to those who sense and better predict the change rate and can exploit it to innovate their products and services. How they find the right timing is the subject of our next chapter.

Actionable Takeaways

Elevate your view—find the two key progress sight lines to conquer confusion. The first line of progress is to exploit the opportunity of *increased data resolution*—to see what's happening in your world in more detail than ever before. The second is to exploit the opportunity to *exert more precision response and digital control* over the things happening moment to moment in your world.

Set a default strategy assumption—deep digital disruption will happen to all. Digital disruption will impact *all* industries, including yours. Remove all complacency, particularly if you are in a stable, old, physical product sector unaccustomed to digital change. Require your team and your peers to justify their beliefs if they think it cannot or will not happen in your sector.

Brainstorm the ways in which the resolution revolution could transform your products. Apply thinking about sensors and the data they create. Think about cloud-connected products and how they can be remotely controlled or updated. Think about the additional services value that could be created by your company or others.

Make digital a core competency—it will become part of what you do. Digital and information technology are no longer just supporting tools for managing your business; digital can penetrate into and completely differentiate your products and services. If you don't take up the opportunity, someone else will.

Plan for instability as Moore's law enters your previously slow-moving industry. Transitioning to an era of nonlinear innovation will be a challenge to many stable management systems and cultures. The period of instability will be sustained. This is not a one-time move. Companies will trump and re-trump each other.

3

Catch the Triple Tipping Point

Three progress dimensions of digital disruption—technology, culture, and regulation—intertwine. Each advances with a different cadence, and the morphing triple tipping point effect that arises creates a daunting compounded uncertainty for many. However, digital leaders know how to exploit opportunity in the face of uncertainty. They keep a sharp eye on the key tipping points. They nudge each one in their favor by constantly probing the edges of the digital frontier. Then, when the time is very nearly right, they move boldly to exploit new industry market space opportunities.

Exploit Compound Uncertainty

In the 1980s, the ordinary citizens of Seoul, South Korea, helped plant many trees in a new park in the central area of the city as part of project to plant ten million trees across the country.[1] For decades, the people of South Korea have been organized and committed to creating an advanced society. Next door to the park is a sprawling modern hospital campus that shares those nationally ambitious aims of being as advanced as any in the world.

Dr. Hee Hwang, chief information officer and chief medical officer at Seoul National University Bundang Hospital, a research and teaching hospital, is on a mission to apply digital techniques to improve the health-care outcomes in his country. "We were the first to use big data analysis on fifteen years of hospital information. For example, a pediatric neurologist can retrieve all kinds of clinically relevant data, including imaging data, electroencephalographic data, demographic data, and all kinds of other social data to make some of the clinical research," he said.

Dr. Hwang wants his hospital to be the first to use new technology because that's one of three critical innovation uncertainties that often gets resolved in his country first.[2] As he pointed out, "South Korea is a very famous country for its strong IT infrastructure and Internet usage." South Korea has the world's highest average Internet connection speed,[3] more than 82 percent of the population is online,[4] and two of the world's biggest mobile device manufacturers, LG and Samsung, operate in its midst. Dr. Hwang sometimes has the opportunity to be first in the world to use the Internet to innovate in digital health care, because his country has crossed a tipping point that others have not.

Judging the market and knowing when a key tipping point is approaching is an important skill for a digital business leader. Launching prematurely and trying to run ahead of technology penetration and acceptance can be painful, expensive, and brand tarnishing. For example, in the summer of 2008 a major British insurance company, Norwich Union, cancelled one of its most talked-about and innovative new products. The BBC reported the product had attracted barely 10 percent of the hoped for 100,000 users.[5] Norwich Union had spent several years developing a complex and revolutionary new form of driving insurance for U.K. motorists called "pay as you drive."[6] By location-tracking a car's movements, the insurer could calculate the risk factor on a moment-by-moment basis and charge per minute like a cell phone service. It was an impressive glimpse into the digital business future. But the product came too soon. The GPS tracker box was expensive, and consumers were a bit spooked by it.[7] The company put the idea on ice for four years, but it did not give up on the premise. As we will see later, the company eventually addressed the same digital opportunity very successfully but in a different way—one that consumers were more ready to accept.

Organizations such as Seoul National University Bungdang Hospital do their best to avoid premature launch. Dr. Hwang and his colleagues have been learning how to test and judge the three key tipping points that separate the premature period, in which failure is probable, from the time when success is likely; these tipping points involve technology, regulation, and culture.

The technology tipping point entails not just the existence of the appropriate technology but its penetration and usage rate. For example, by 2012 in Korea, more than 60 percent of people older than fifty years of age and more than 38 percent of people older than sixty were Internet users.[8] This helped Seoul National University Bundang Hospital successfully prove a new kind of digital home-health support never seen before.

The hospital showed that a chronic disease such as diabetes could be managed remotely at home, without unnecessary hospital visits. The hospital provided connected glucometers that used wireless technology to collect blood sugar level data while patients were at home. The data was then sent over the network to the hospital's health-care information system. "We applied a rules-based clinical decision support system to assess it," Dr. Hwang said. The system contacts the patient if the glucose level is abnormal compared with the level set by the physicians or nurses. "After a one-year period of the project, we proved that trial system patients regulate their glucose level mostly better compared with the non-involved patients," he said.[9]

Many nations have aging populations and medical care cost problems that could be managed in part through such advances, and South Korea is using technology as soon as it becomes possible. But, as Dr. Hwang pointed out, there are other tipping points that impact viability, such as regulation: "The older medical institutions in South Korea are controlled by the government regulations, and usually these legal or regulatory principles move slowly compared with the speed of the changes of technology. For example, according to the state of South Korea, the public can visit the hospital without any kind of (medical professional) referral note. That can increase hospital costs."[10]

Finally, there is culture. Even if the technology works and regulations can accommodate it, people have to feel comfortable with the idea. That doesn't apply only to the technology itself—it is complicated by broader societal issues, as Dr. Hwang explained: "South Korea and some Far East countries have a long history of some herbal medicine or some Oriental medicine, so there are some conflicts between two different types of the medical service to the public. Western [scientific] medicine was adopted one hundred or two hundred years ago, but we have a long history of more than a thousand years, so actually there is still some confusion or some misleading publications about modern medicine to the public."

Then, of course, there is always the issue of privacy. As Dr. Hwang notes, "Medical information is one of the top privacy and security-required fields, so there is some lack of the social consensus to use the technologies, especially the difficult technologies in the medical health-care sector."

These cultural barriers resolve at different speeds in different places. In the U.K., for example, society has been adjusting quickly in the area of data privacy. Today, many more people are comfortable trading a bit of location data for some benefit—for instance, they readily download mobile apps that show local weather forecasts for where they are standing. By 2012, consumer culture had changed sufficiently to support a new kind of car insurance. Aviva (previously named Norwich Union) returned to the same basic idea of digitally measuring a driver's risk, but this time it introduced a smartphone app instead.[11] Now the "tracker box" cost the company nothing because it used the customer's own location- and acceleration-sensing smartphone. Data was not collected live but over a period of time to measure average risk behavior, and the benefit was a 20 percent discount rather than a per-minute bill. Aviva's result included a successful metric of more than 230,000 downloads by mid 2014.[12]

The uncertainties of technology advances, regulatory changes, and cultural shifts combine and compound to make it very hard for a leader to decide when to make a major digital business innovation move. However, a company can't just sit on its hands until the time is obviously ripe, because a bold start-up might steal the opportunity and the market.

Compound Uncertainty Hangs on the Triple Tipping Point

Digital business leaders must account for three crucial factors when trying to estimate the timing of markets and digital changes: technology progress, cultural evolution, and regulatory developments. When all three come into alignment, new markets are created, and they often grow suddenly and very rapidly. The leader's task is to estimate when that will happen and to be ready to take advantage when it does.

You don't have to be perfect at getting the timing right. Often, that's simply not possible. To win, you have to be a bit better than the competition. It will be important to identify and work on *all three* tipping points that are key to industry competitiveness. In technology, take care not to underestimate or get caught out by the nonlinear pace of change. In culture, evaluate social acceptability and keep testing its boundaries without crossing the "creepy line." With regulation, innovate because of it or in spite of it, treating it as a potential source of opportunity, not just an obstacle. The best digital leaders work to nudge one or more of the three tipping points in their favor.

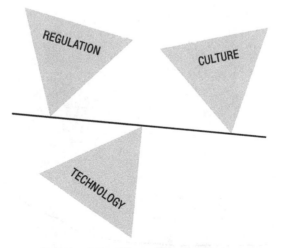

FIGURE 3.1 The Three Tipping Points

The Compounding of Uncertainties

The three issues of technology, culture, and regulation have interdependencies that can compound the problem of estimating when a new product or service idea will take off. Let's review a U.K. episode from the first decade of the 2000s, to see how these dynamics played out in fashion retail e-commerce. Initial dot-com exuberance fuelled premature start-ups that failed completely. For example, online fashion retailer Boo.com burned through over $100 million of venture capital before going bust,[13] a story of failure so compelling a book was written about it.[14] Today, however, online fashion is mainstream and is a key high-growth element in most clothing retailers' business strategies, from H&M and Zara to Burberry and Hugo Boss. What changed?

The second generation of online specialty fashion start-ups, such as ASOS and Net-a-Porter, had to work out when the triple tipping point would arrive. The sales curve for ASOS shows the characteristic hockey stick shape.

From 2000 to 2007 sales were fairly flat. In 2007, they reached the triple tipping point. Technology, shopping culture, and regulation aligned, leading many more consumers to want to buy clothes online.

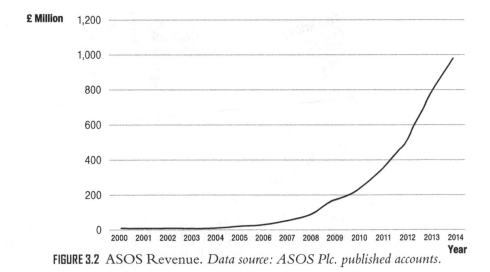

FIGURE 3.2 ASOS Revenue. *Data source: ASOS Plc. published accounts.*

By 2010, mainstream retailers like H&M and Zara followed with their own major online strategies.[15]

First, the resolution revolution came. High-speed broadband and high-resolution computer screens let shoppers see important clothing details such as buttons, stitching, and weave. This simply wasn't possible in the days of dial-up Internet. E-commerce tracking systems allowed retailers and their logistics providers precise control over time-boxed deliveries and returns processes.

Second, the culture changed. Women's desire to shop online increased. In the advanced economies, women did not match men in their use of the web until 2000, and their e-commerce uptake took longer.[16] For online fashion retail to succeed, it was essential that women browse and shop online habitually.

Third, the regulations evolved. Distance selling regulations assured consumers of particular rights online that they enjoyed offline, such as the right to return goods. Clarifications from financial regulators regarding online credit cards use, without fear of different or additional fraud liabilities, also helped. Today, online fashion shopping is commonplace, growing, and unremarkable, because some companies got the triple tipping point right. Others died trying before conditions were ripe.

In our U.K. fashion story, the three tipping points seem simple. However, these key uncertainty factors are not mutually exclusive. Sometimes they can impact one another, causing complex compounding of the problems for business planners. For example, a simple technology change can make an idea more compelling to consumers, overcoming their cultural reticence.

In 2014, American fashion house Tory Burch created a collection of attractive jewelry-like accessories that wrap around Fitbit wearable fitness activity trackers.[17] Not every woman thinks a bright plastic gadget looks good on her wrist, and the Tory Burch products successfully hide and glamorize the technology, making them more attractive for a portion of the market. This kind of tipping point "nudge" doesn't happen by serendipity. It requires leaders who carve out strong competencies within their firms and who are determined to keep experimenting and pushing the edge.

Working at the heart of the fashion trade in New York City, Mike Giresi, chief information officer at Tory Burch, is one of those leaders. "I think people can move so much faster than companies in terms of embracing new technology and changing behavior," he told us. The Fitbit accessories were an example of taking that cultural risk. "We did not know how people were going to respond," Giresi said. "We felt pretty good about it, but again, you never know. When we went live with the product we exceeded demand by four times in terms of sales. We actually sold out in two and a half hours. So that's something that would have never happened in a company that was not thinking about risk orientation, how they expand the brand, how to take it in different places and just allowing tech to lead versus be a follower, or potentially even worse, simply a cost center."[18]

Tipping Point 1: Technology

Don't underestimate the nonlinear pace of change. As the American–Canadian speculative fiction author William Gibson once remarked, "The future is already here—it's just not very evenly distributed."[19]

All around us we read of technologies and ideas that are seemingly here and not here at the same time. You see news images of drone delivery trials by big companies like Amazon, Alibaba, and DHL, but when will it actually happen? You can buy a hobby-grade 3D printer for a few thousand bucks, and yet nothing you have in your home today is manufactured using that technology. When will 3D technology start to change mainstream consumer products?

Online shoe retailer Zappos is consistently rated one of America's most admired companies by customers and other business leaders. Senior director of corporate applications John Peretiatko explains that 3D technology is being reviewed by the company for the role it might play in a radically different future for the footwear industry: "Some phones now have the capability of doing 3D imaging. There are companies out there working on using that 3D imaging technology to create a customized size and fit. Basically, a customer takes a 3D image of their foot, and we can do something on our side to do the same thing with how a shoe will fit. You mash those two things up together and you get a better idea of how something is going to fit."

Peretiatko didn't mention them, but we note that start-ups like Volumental and FitFully are already beginning to do this measurement. It's amazing what the resolution revolution can make better. We have always measured the length of our feet, but seldom width and never height.

Speaking about the full dimensions of the foot, Peretiatko said, "That's not captured anywhere right now, so customers have no idea when they're ordering something how it's going to fit them. 3D imagery is in its infancy right now, but two, three years from now, there's going to be another way to look at the size and fit of footwear."[20] Will it take two years or three years? Notice that Peretiatko and his colleagues are keeping track of technology's advance, continuously testing and reestimating when these things will become possible. That's how digital leaders probe the edge.

This technology tipping point conundrum, which has previously been restricted to "tech" companies, now extends to all companies because the next generation of everyday products will likely include digital capability.

Moore's law and related progress rates for memory, bandwidth, and screen technology price-performance improvement are quite predictable but they are not linear. So a business leader without a technology background who is accustomed to straight-line extrapolation can easily be caught out. Additionally, the following key dimensions all drive the pace of change toward a technology tipping point.

Industrialization. Cloud computing's factory-style economies of scale propel price performance acceleration of computing and storage, blasting through new tipping points.

Consumerization. Many of the boldest, most imaginative, and lowest-cost new technologies are developed for consumer markets first (e.g., high-definition TV screens). For business leaders, the tipping point issue might be finding the first secure, high-reliability version for corporate use.

Democratization. New development tools make app programming, electronics, and other technologies directly accessible to enthusiastic amateurs and non-tech professionals. The tipping point might come from the creativity of different minds.

Globalization. All over the world, governments, engineers, and entrepreneurs are collaborating to create their own Silicon Valley–style tech enclaves. The tipping point might arise anywhere—not just California, Bangalore, or Seoul but perhaps from Reykjavik, Tel Aviv, or Helsinki.

Data analytics and smart machines. Technology feeds on itself and gets smarter. Learning algorithms discover trends in the masses of data on the Internet. They parse language, perform sentiment analysis, and make predictive forecasts. This machine intelligence helps find the next tipping point.

Overall, technology may be the easiest tipping point to predict but the hardest to change. As a leader, you are dependent on a very complex R&D, capital investment, and technology supply chain. Multibillion-dollar bets placed by companies like Intel and ARM will decide where the silicon goes next and how fast it gets there. This, then, is the most independent variable of the three. However, it can be influenced to some degree.

Digital business innovation doesn't rest on a single technology. Usually, a combination of technologies is crucial for successful development, and one or more of those technologies will often be highly specialized. Leaders can sometimes accelerate that process by nudging just one technology and allowing the market to move the rest—then the whole opportunity falls into place. Babolat did this when developing its first digital tennis racquet. The Bluetooth connectivity, mobile app, and cloud data storage were standard elements, but for Babolat's racquet, the tipping point technology was in the tiny specialized sensors. For those, the company reached out via business networks to partner with a local start-up called Movea, which traces its high-tech origins to the research end of the French nuclear industry.[21]

Tipping Point 2: Culture

Balance new value propositions with the "creepy line." Technology can test and challenge our cultural and social boundaries. Often, we yield because the new opportunities it brings are worth the change. But the rate of cultural change is not evenly spread across countries, communities, and social groups.

For the 2012 Summer Olympics held in London, the city needed new secure street litter bins that would deal with millions of visitors' trash yet not provide a ready-made receptacle for terrorists' bombs. A new company formed to provide the bins, betting that it could make money selling advertising on the side of them. Each bin had a TV screen built into it on which glossy, magazine-like images were displayed, interspersed with live local travel information to catch the eye of both Olympics visitors and commuting office workers anxious to catch their train home.[22] It was an exciting and impressive example of the creative business models that digital technology can enable. But in 2013, a step beyond what our Gartner colleague Frank Buytendijk calls the "creepy line" caused the fledgling company significant negative press and problems.

The trash bins were enabled to listen for the unique MAC address codes that every passing laptop, tablet, and smartphone offers up when hunting for Wi-Fi access.[23] Using this data to estimate the number of unique passersby who saw the ads on the bins would let advertisers measure the impressions and value the service. But it also could make people feel spied upon in a public place. The local governing authority, called the City of London Corporation, decided it was a privacy-invading step too far, and it required the company to stop such tracking.[24]

Yet at the same time, in another part of Europe, the same kind of tracking operated and nobody seemed to mind. Since 2011, Copenhagen Airport users with Wi-Fi enabled on their devices, have had their location tracked as they walked through the terminal buildings.[25] The company that operates the airport uses the data to offer passengers a helpful location-finding app and to analyze passenger-flow patterns for planning purposes.[26] Maybe Copenhagen's tracking is accepted because the tracked person can gain a direct benefit if she chooses the app, or maybe it's because an airport is a different kind of public space than a London city street—either way, this tracking seems to be accepted.

We share many things quite openly online today that we would not have discussed with or in front of strangers in the past. Examples include political views, photos of ourselves, and location data. In the end, this kind of change and the likely tipping points within it will be a qualitative judgment call and risk bet that a leader has to make, not a mathematical calculation. However, culture can be shifted by the best marketers: the right phrase can diffuse a social tension point and the right celebrity endorsement can cause enough early adopters to join a bandwagon. The best way to judge the culture is to observe it.

Roger Liew, chief technology officer at e-commerce travel site Orbitz, recalled how he spotted the tipping point for mobile just by observing people during his daily commute to the office: "In 2011, I believe the percentage of our mobile transactions for hotels was less than 1 or 2 percent. Then, in the span of two years, it exceeded 20 percent." The company was prescient in developing for the trend in 2010. "I remember just living life and thinking the percentage of people that I see on my commute that have their noses in their phones or that are browsing something seems to be increasing, and employees of the company couldn't live without their devices," Liew shared.[27] Sometimes searching for the cultural tipping point is a little more methodical, however.

In 2008, Hidemi Harada-san, a young manager in the corporate marketing and planning department at Tokio Marine & Nichido Fire Insurance Co. Ltd., participated in an idea competition within the product development department. One day he was with two women, one in her mid-twenties and the other in her mid-thirties. The woman in her thirties commented that she felt "cumbersome" when she met insurance agents to make a contract. She wanted a handier and more convenient way to purchase insurance, one that was "like buying candies at convenience store." This comment rang Harada-san's bell, but his colleagues didn't see the need for it. "How much revenue can we expect from the small amount of insurance?" they inquired. Clearly, they didn't yet see the cultural tipping point.

Harada-san conducted market research, and at the same time he did a wildcat survey at a university with the help of a professor who specialized in marketing. To Harada-san's surprise, the university students had more interest in insurance than the insurance company expected. They had concerns about driving their parents' or a friend's car without insurance coverage, for example. Harada-san collected those voices to justify his idea. He also organized an idea competition with students about how to best sell this new type of insurance. The result was Tokio Marine's innovative One Day Auto Insurance, which allows buyers to purchase daily insurance via their mobile devices. It would have been easy to miss this cultural tipping point brought about by a growing demographic, the millennial generation, that was ready for a new type of product enabled by existing technology. Culture can be hard to judge, but you can measure it by testing ideas in focus groups or via social media.

The challenge with the cultural tipping point around technology advancement is that it is contextual and difficult to predict with certainty. However, the timing of the tipping point in a national culture can come down to a window of just a few short years.

Mike Bracken, executive director of digital and chief data officer, U.K. government, said that the creation of the government digital service (GDS) was driven by multiple culture shifts. First, Internet use reached a tipping point in 2006, and by 2010 a strong set of unmet demands existed, namely that people wanted better service. Second, government was spending too much money. "We'd just had a financial crash and there was a strong demand to fix that," Bracken said. "The third factor was internal—people were sick and tired of the internal tools they were given to do their jobs inside government. The fourth factor was a political policy factor," he continued. "Politicians were tired of not being able to get things done digitally quickly enough. The fifth was a risk factor—an ongoing steady drip, drip, drip of IT failures meant there was a perception that something had to change. Never before had all those five factors been aligned. We'd had periods where one or more of those factors were in play, never all five. That's why there was openness to doing something new."[28]

Tipping Point 3: Regulation

In 2014, the U.S. Federal Aviation Administration published its first rules for the commercial use of aerial drones in U.S. airspace. These rules were just a start, however, and much more research and regulatory development will follow in the months and years to come. The rules were prompted by the actions of both small and large players: media companies want to use drones to take sports and news video; farmers want to use drones to survey their crops. Perhaps what hurried the discussion most, though, was Amazon's release in late 2013 of a video demonstrating drone-based delivery of e-commerce packages to customers' homes.

A limiting factor is the legal right to fly drones over public and private spaces. At what height should drones operate to avoid buildings yet also stay clear of aircraft? What precautions are needed to stop them from colliding or falling from the sky and injuring people? How will registration and insurance work? There are many questions to answer, and ultimately the matter is a complex game of *comparative* risk judgment. After all, motorcycle pizza delivery isn't exactly the safest method of transport. National aviation regulators of countries suddenly find themselves challenged to evolve safe operating rules and techniques that might enable a new high-growth industry and a structural efficiency in the way our urban societies operate. New lobbying groups, including the Association for Unmanned Vehicle Systems International and the Drone Pilots Association, are springing up to try to negotiate a way for the technology to make its way safely into our lives.

However, any industry that might be negatively impacted by drones' capabilities can't just hope the technology will be blocked by regulators, because start-ups like DJI (Da-Jiang Innovations) will find ways to change the game. In 2006, DJI was founded in China, and by 2015 it had become the world's number-one manufacturer of drones specializing in still photography and video. Smaller than your wastebasket, with an HD camera slung underneath, these GPS-tracked, digitally stabilized, and remote-controlled devices sell for under $1,500. They have proven so popular that the company grew from fifty employees to more than fifteen hundred between 2011 and 2014.[29] But, wait, aren't drones illegal?

It depends on the country, and, like many digital innovations, from autonomous cars to electronic cigarettes, the situation is fuzzy. DJI spokesperson Michael Perry said the company tries to ease the technology adoption country by country by finding ways for users to follow proper rules for drone use. For example, when the company sells drones in Australia and New Zealand, Perry said, "You get that pamphlet that says, 'You can do this, you can't do that.' We think that sets a really clear tone for what's acceptable in terms of best safe flying practices, and if you don't follow these practices, here are the consequences."[30]

These new entities change the game by reshaping the rules at the edge of what digital technology has made both doable and economical—and your company is competing with them. Who might lose where DJI is gaining? Helicopter service companies and aerial photography companies, for a start. And if DJI makes photo drones common and acceptable, who is to say it won't try pizza delivery next?

In recent history, regulator intervention has often proven a crucial tipping point for the development and evolution of many digital business advances, as shown by the examples in Figure 3.3.

Regulation is often seen as a barrier, but it can be treated as an enabler. New technology can be positioned in a way that circumvents existing regulation. For example, in the early days of e-cigarettes it wasn't clear whether they would be treated as a medical device or as tobacco. It wasn't clear whether laws designed to prevent smoking in offices would apply to "vaping." And it wasn't clear how advertising rules applied. So trailblazing companies were able to make the market for e-cigs while the regulators deliberated.

Lack of regulation also acted as an enabler for India's Bharatiya Janata Party (BJP) party through the 2014 multi-stage election process. Arvind Gupta of the BJP told us, "During the first few semi-finals we had very little regulation because the regulators didn't understand social media. We were the only one using it so interactively. In the last

Period	Regulatory Action	Impact
1990s	Text message interoperability between mobile phone carriers is required by various national telecommunications regulators.	Massive, high-profit margin consumer text messaging services market is created.
2000s	U.S. Digital Millennium Copyright Act makes it illegal to circumvent digital rights management technology.	It enables large companies to develop digital music and film distribution methods without fear of completely losing market control.
2010s	EU distance selling regulations to protect consumer rights are passed.	It raises consumer confidence and the scale and growth rate of e-commerce markets.
2010s	Regulators in many countries encourage a shift from analog to digital TV by organized, sometimes auctioned, frequency spectrum allocations.	It results in the "digital dividend" of freed-up VHF (ex analog TV) frequencies for other mobile phone and data use.
2010s	California DMV evolves progressive autonomous vehicle regulation.	It enables Google, Tesla and others to develop and test self-driving cars — a likely industry disruption.
2010s	Major tobacco companies encourage the U.S. FDA to hasten the development of electronic cigarette regulations.	Digital and electronic "vaping" market will accelerate as regulation becomes clearer.
2010s	"The right to be forgotten" is asserted by EU authorities on search engines.	The impact is not yet clear; privacy rights clarification might lift consumer confidence.
2010s	International mobile telco representative organization proposes and lobbies for "mobile money"-enabling regulation.	Peer-to-peer mobile-phone-based solutions can make electronic distance payment available to the very large "unbanked" markets.
2010s	U.S. Federal Commodity Futures Trading Commission argues for flexible regulation of emerging digital currencies.	It enables orderly rapid development of more bitcoin-like currencies.

FIGURE 3.3 How Regulation Shifts Digital Markets

stage, they brought some norms for social media under the election guideline, but still they were very vague."

Gupta saw working ahead of regulation as a general opportunity for innovators, and pointed out that it's what companies such as Airbnb and Uber have done: "Is Airbnb a hotel room provider or an aggregator? No regulation, no policy can keep pace. Before the legislator and the policymakers can decide, [innovators] come up with a new business model and start operating differently. Such is the advantage of digital. I'm not saying we should use it in a wrong manner, what I'm saying is it gives you the flexibility to be one step ahead rather than failing on policy implications[31]." In chapter 6, we'll describe in greater detail how the BJP took digital to the core of the party's efforts.

At Allied Irish banks, CEO David Duffy was determined to drive global-class digital innovation. He saw the regulatory territory in and around banking as very fluid, which opened up opportunities for him, his direct conventional competitors, and new entrants. "I think regulation is an interesting concept now because of a dramatic reregulation which is dealing with only 40 percent of the banking industry," he told us. "We need to see how that plays out, and that's a competitive restriction. But on top of that, the telco industry and the technology industries in payments are not (banking) regulated, so it's a massively imbalanced world. If you take the entire technology industry and the retail industry and the banking industry converging, there's no regulator that has a purview which is sufficiently large."[32]

One day a tipping point might be reached at which the existing regulators will be restructured as these different sectors start to merge and blur. That might be a moment of business opportunity.

True Leaders Constantly Probe the Digital Frontier

Google is an obvious example of a company that is always testing the edges of what's feasible and permissible. For example, its Google Glass augmented-reality eyewear device, first discussed in 2012 and made available in small quantities in 2013, was an exciting new technology that caught the imagination of consumers and businesspeople the world over. But by December 2014 it didn't seem to be working out, and the company withdrew it from sale.[33] As the *New York Times* explained in an article, tech reviewers had criticized the product's battery life and bugs, and had raised the obvious privacy concerns. And the public wasn't ready. The *Times* noted the device had been banned from bars, theaters, casinos, and other public venues.[34]

Technology problems, cultural problems related to privacy, and local regulatory problems: Google was on the early side of all three major tipping points. However, there are signs that the company won't give up on the idea.[35] The time wasn't right, so it will regroup and start again. Just as Norwich Union/Aviva did with its car insurance idea, Google will keep probing the bounds of technology, regulation, and cultural acceptance. And it should, because the idea of augmented-reality eyewear has in fact already found a mainstream consumer use, albeit a niche one. Since 2012, sunglasses and sportswear maker Oakley has successfully sold luxury $650 augmented-reality ski goggles called Airwave, which do many of the same things Google Glass did, such as overlaying location information in the user's field of view.[36] Oakley, part of the Luxottica group of companies, has advanced its digital business by finding one space in the triple tipping point envelope that is just a bit more open to an early move. Its probing of the digital frontier was successful.

True leaders accept that perfect prediction is a fool's game. Instead, they use repeated, innovation-based market testing to probe the rapidly moving edges of the technological, regulatory, and cultural tipping points. They look for and push for the point at which introducing new products and services successfully is just possible. Norwich Union/Aviva experimented, failed, learned, and successfully launched a new product with a similar proposition. Orbitz spotted the signs of widespread mobile use and evolved its travel service for mobile e-commerce. Tokio Marine created an environment where it could seed ideas and conducted the research necessary to spot a demographic need for one-day car insurance.

Actionable Takeaways

Identify and work on *all three* tipping points key to industry competitiveness. Actively track specific technological, social, and regulatory tipping points that have the potential to impact your competitive situation. Focusing on just the technology change and failing to address social and regulatory aspects will lead to dangerous blind spots.

Don't underestimate the nonlinear pace of technology change. The pace of technology-enabled change will continue to accelerate, fuelled by its own "combinatorial engine" effect across technology domains. Leaders from traditional industries should not underestimate how fast the art of what is technically possible can tip, nor its disruptive power. Sometimes the change just ahead of you feels like science fiction.

Evaluate cultural acceptance, balancing new value propositions against the "creepy line." Push the limits but do it gently. It's easy to take a step too far, as in the case of London's trash bins. If you face an uphill battle, don't be too proud to withdraw, regroup, and reconsider, as Google has done with Google Glass. Or find a niche where the culture is more accepting—like the ski culture that happily tolerates Oakley's special-purpose augmented-reality eyewear. Or try a location where people are just a little more accepting—like the confines of Copenhagen's airport buildings.

Innovate because of, or in spite, of regulation. Regulation often moves slowly, but it can still be a source of opportunity. Technology can be used to avoid existing regulation and create products or services that meet market needs in a way that's not yet bound by regulation. Your understanding of and relationship with regulators may be the advantage you have over less knowledgeable start-ups. As we saw in chapter 1, Eric Babolat petitioned the International Tennis Federation for a change in the rules of the game so his revolutionary new digital product could be accepted.

Nudge one of the three tipping points in your favor. While macro tipping points are outside most people's control, digital leaders seek to understand them while nudging one specific point for their advantage. Help a venture capitalist incubate a key subtechnology, lead an industry lobbying initiative to win a progressive regulation change, or help shape consumer culture rather than be blocked by it.

4

Whose Industry Is It Anyway?

Digital business fundamentally changes the core of products and services. The value that customers experience often becomes more data centric and digitally controlled. Both the competencies required to create that value and the pathways to its delivery are unusual, challenging, and often resisted. However, once companies engage and start to develop the new competencies and pathways, their power and attractiveness often grows quickly. Traditional players that have enjoyed dominance for decades can find others suddenly seizing these new routes. The walls that once defended one industry from another crumble and become blurred and ill defined. Defending your old core won't do; instead, go after the new opportunities and build your part of the new platform before someone else uses it to control your business.

Five floors up, in modern offices on the Champs-Élysées, Maurice Levy, the CEO of Publicis Groupe, has a sweeping view across some of the richest city blocks of Paris and down toward the Seine. Founded in 1926, Publicis is one of the "big four" advertising agencies, with $8 billion in revenue. It has acquired many smaller agencies over the decades of innovation that led from radio and TV to the web and Facebook. Now the company needs to increase its digital competencies, and it is both creating and buying them. Its 2014 acquisition of Sapient brought Publicis the technology consulting capabilities it needed to compete with companies such as Accenture, which have traditionally been labeled a separate sector.

"Blur is the key word in this world. There is a blur in everything," Levy said. "There is a blur in the boundaries when it comes to verticals. There is a blur in the role of the company."[1] Levy isn't just reflecting on the clients of his agency business, he has been rethinking his own company too. Levy was born in the 1940s, and his path to the CEO role was an unusual one. He joined his company as its IT director in 1971. His age and experience give him the wisdom to see the current wave of technology change in its proper historical context.

"We used to live in a world where we would categorize companies and industries, even people, in kind of formatted ways," Levy said. "This person is an engineer. That company operates in the automobile industry. These days, everything is blurred: people are blurred, companies are blurred, even time is blurred. Think of a company like Amazon. What kind of a company is it? A bookseller? A retailer? A media outlet? The great thing about that is that we can now think about the intersections in a way that we never thought of before. Today you can be very creative and successful in redefining these blurred lines."[2]

Levy's slightly incredulous tone is not inspired by Amazon alone. Publicis interacts with many of the world's largest brands as they seek to map their digital journeys. Other, lesser-known companies are blurring things even more. "Everyone is starting to worry about being 'Ubered.' It's the idea that you suddenly wake up to find your legacy business gone...clients have never been so confused or concerned about their brands or their business model," said Levy.[3]

This boundary-blurring force doesn't just affect information and services industries. It is directly impacting physical product industries, too. Indeed, it can even blur the line between media and vehicle manufacturing.

In early 2014, Carlos Ghosn, CEO of Renault-Nissan said, "Not only will autonomous driving enhance safety but it will also free up time for drivers. Being connected will enable them to make the most of this extra time by providing them with access to new in-car services such as video conferences, online shopping, travel information, and more."[4]

Ghosn was pointing to the possibility of a fuzzy future in the 2020s, when the car industry might need to make more of its money from digital services provided to vehicles and less from making and selling the vehicles themselves. It is not entirely clear who will have the greatest control over the movies or business services streaming in and out of the self-driving cars. But Nissan, Volkswagen, and Ford didn't kick off that self-driving future—Google did. At every turn, it now seems that anyone can enter any industry, using digital as a vector.

Boundaries Are Blurred by Digital Substitution

In the early 2000s, a new breed of powerful online travel intermediaries sprang up, including Orbitz. These sites provided quick price comparison via sophisticated cloud-based algorithmic systems. Today, these players continue to use digital skills in an attempt to keep ahead of the more traditional players in their industries—the airlines and hotels—but even the newcomers have to work hard not be disrupted themselves.

Sitting in the sleek, glassy towers that arch over Ogilvie rail station in downtown Chicago, Roger Liew, chief technology officer of Orbitz, is very aware of the challenge. He must use all of his software engineering and algorithm skills to stay ahead. "It is brutally competitive," he shared. "One of the challenges is that you don't know where the competitors are going to come from. In a fairly short span of time, Airbnb is on everybody's radar. The reason it's so competitive is because there's not a lot of switching costs for online customers. If you don't satisfy their demands today, it's fairly easy for them to switch to a competitor. That's what compels us to build something that is world class. If you stop focusing on that it puts you just a step behind."[5]

In the new digital business game, the very core of industries is being challenged and reinvented. For example, if you need to get from point A to point B, you don't require a taxi—you just need a car and a driver. Uber realized that and created a service that many consumers feel is better, using digital services to orchestrate alternative assets such as ordinary people and their cars. If you are visiting a city, you have to sleep in a bed, but that doesn't mean it has to be in a hotel room. Airbnb realized that and substituted people's spare bedrooms, moored boats, and RVs. Customer needs are being met in different, and often better, ways.

As physical products become connected, we will see a lot more of these substitutions and customer value improvement solutions. When a product becomes connected it can be remotely tracked and manipulated or utilized. The resolution revolution means this will happen with ever more detailed clarity and precision, providing a powerful means for substituting the products and services people enjoy with better digital versions. But the competencies required to master those newer products and services are also new. They come from other domains, like the technology industry itself. The traditional core competencies of existing companies often become less like industry-defending fortresses and more like deadweight. That's what is happening in the car industry.

Once a self-driving car is a possibility, the old competencies of shaping metal and optimizing combustion engine performance become relatively less important to customers making purchase decisions. What were once capabilities that differentiated a business can become commodity costs. To replace the original core competencies, organizations need strong competencies in software, algorithms, online connected services management, and services creativity.

At Volvo Cars in Gothenburg, Sweden, CIO Klas Bendrik understands this fundamental shift. In addition to the company's development of a digital one-time key, Volvo Cars is developing a number of highly creative autonomous vehicle services package ideas—all of them to drive customer value. One example of all these ideas is to enable your car to turn itself around on your driveway to be ready for tomorrow's commute. Another might let your car drive its way out of a supermarket parking lot, to pick you up, just at the moment you leave the door laden with groceries. These ideas seem radical but they are forged from within his deep understanding of how much industries will be changed and boundaries blurred: "Around the world, people are more seldom wanting to actually hold a driving license or own a car. They would like to get access to transportation. We have mega cities where basically it will be very difficult to have your own vehicle. A number of these mega trends are impacting us as an automotive company. People in Volvo Cars have acknowledged that step by step and more and more."[6]

At Babolat, CEO Eric Babolat has connected a piece of sports equipment with the ability to analyze and store sensor data for customers. The services he later develops may become as important as his company's previous capabilities, such a finding better materials for handles and strings. "The platform of opportunities [the connected racquet] gives for the brand, for the player, and for everyone is just huge,"[7] he said.

As Babolat customers evolve with the product, they may want online services to monitor their children's playing performance data as their games develop over time. Is that still racquet making—or would the company invade a coach's business? Moving down that path could be viewed as a distraction from core business, crossing the boundary into some other industry. It should also cause leaders to reconsider what industry they are really in.

At Orbitz, company leaders have to think hard about that question, and CTO Roger Liew has one perspective. "I believe first and foremost we are a travel company that is focused on using technology to help people plan and book travel," he said. "On the flipside, my CEO actually believes we're a technology company that happens to focus on travel."[8]

That duality is a really important maturing stage in the digital business leader's mind-set. Whatever industry you operate in traditionally, your company, like Orbitz, Volvo, and Babolat, should think of itself as a technology company too. Amazon wins by being both a retailer and a tech company, and Uber wins by being both a taxi company and a tech company. If new companies could use that duality to cross a blurred boundary and tear a hole in the side of your industry, you'd better learn how to do that too.

At Gartner, we have a simple way of repeatedly expressing this radical shift until it becomes common thinking: every company is a technology company.

Every Company Is a Technology Company

Some business leaders already agree. Irish banker David Duffy worked at Goldman Sachs, ING, and Standard Bank before becoming chief executive of Allied Irish Banks (AIB). Here's how he put it: "You just have to recognize that we are most likely going to be a highly-technology-driven technology utility in the business of payment and cash management, and if that's the great portion of the volume of our activity in retail, what's different about that versus how Google operates?"[9]

In a *Financial Times* article, Francisco González, CEO of Spanish and international bank BBVA, explained why banks must become part of what he calls the BIT industry (banking, information, and technology): "Some bankers and analysts think that Google, Facebook, Amazon, or the like will not fully enter a highly regulated, low-margin business such as banking. I disagree. What is more, I think banks that are not prepared for such new competitors face certain death."[10]

So is every industry going to be subsumed into the "tech" sector? Not quite, though it might feel like that for a few years. Eventually, a new landscape of digitally empowered and data-enabled industries will evolve, but it will take time for the new shapes to become apparent.

The Challenge Comes from Outside and Underneath

Traditional products being changed by digital—including payments, music, books, and cars—have one thing in common: the companies forcing change most often do not come from within the industry. In the tobacco business, it was a Chinese start-up called Ruyan Group that first marketed the modern electronic and increasingly digital cigarette. Uber has shaken the taxi industry with its crowdsourced virtual asset structure and dynamic marketplace model of private drivers and their cars. Airbnb has shaken the hotel industry with a similar virtual resource model applied to the private room rental marketplace.

These players eat away at the market that the existing players have enjoyed, sometimes for decades, by substituting a better product or service made possible in a digital world. Sometimes the attackers come up from underneath like a shoal of many small piranha fish. The hundreds of small makers of electronic cigarettes and the myriad entrants to the mobile app payments business appeared like this. Other times, the protagonists are big, deeply funded Silicon Valley start-ups or huge tech companies, such as Apple, with its Apple Pay payments system, and Amazon, which redirected the future of the book publishing industry with its Kindle device. As Maurice Levy of Publicis said, "We have a situation where the invasion of digital by someone with a clever mind can disrupt any kind of business. I agree that the Internet of Things is not about the things, it's about products. This is changing quite dramatically."[11]

New Industries Will Emerge from the Blur

A tobacco company manages a number of key operations: an agricultural supply chain for a crop, a factory manufacturing process for cigarettes, marketing, regulatory control, and distribution channels. But what does that company become when it manufactures digital electronic devices that auto-reorder flavored nicotine "juice" that customers "vape," and the company tracks customers' daily consumption activity online? The juice can contain industrially extracted nicotine, so there is almost no tobacco. Maybe the technology will extend to other chemicals. Perhaps we have to call it the vaping services sector.

In another example, the capsule coffee industry will extend into other areas of nutrition, such as tea and baby formula. The world's largest food company, Nestlé, is already starting to do that in some countries with its Special.T and BabyNes systems, and BabyNes is already mobile-app enabled.[12] Meanwhile, the pharmaceutical and medical device industries will be more tightly bound to models that incorporate consumer-grade digital drug delivery devices and sensor-enabled pills.[13]

Perhaps tobacco, functional foods, and pharmaceuticals will start to merge into common online data and services platforms. This is the kind of industry boundary blurring that disrupts and potentially destroys brands. This blurring is already happening between financial services and mobile telecoms, and something similar is happening with sports equipment makers, fitness gadget makers, and the diet industry as all vie for control of our so-called "quantified self" data in the cloud. As we saw in chapter 3, even women's fashion company Tory Burch is now involved with Fitbits. So it seems like everyone is looking to participate in this blurred-boundary digital space. It is a morphing world, where leaders will need to play and win new kinds of cross-industry games and preempt market space invaders.

Sometimes new companies emerge to challenge so many traditional attributes that they simply defy existing industry classification. Take, for example, Shapeways.com. Founded in 2007 and headquartered in New York, with factories in Eindhoven in the Netherlands, Shapeways is a web-based business in which the following activities occur:

- Designers upload 3D CAD models of products such as jewelry and espresso cups.
- Versions in different materials and colors are offered to consumers; prices vary with the material—for example, a green plastic bracelet costs less than one made of silver.
- The chosen item is made for you from raw material by 3D printer and sent to your door.

It's not immediately obvious how to classify this very digital business. Is it an online style catalogue of curated specialty designer objects? Is it a consumer packaged goods (CPG) manufacturer? Is it a retailer? Is it a services broker? Is it an eBay-like transaction fee marketplace? The answer to all of these questions seems to be yes. This quiet company has been making big waves, setting an example that even Walmart and Amazon have paid attention to.

At a 2014 shareholders meeting, Walmart CEO Douglas McMillon addressed his audience while standing in front of a low coffee table. Sitting on it was collection of ten-inch-high plastic figures, each one unique. They were 3D printed models of his executive team. He said, "I'm sure you've heard of 3D printing. We've had some fun in the U.S.

and the U.K. printing items for customers. We can easily imagine a day when we can print small household items or replacement parts in a store or a DC [distribution center]."[14]

Amazon has gone a stage further. In 2014 it launched the Amazon 3D Printing Store,[15] which performs services similar to those of Shapeways. Even the most powerful tech companies must monitor and preempt invaders. Trump and trump again—digital business will be a story of repeated disruptions.

Digital Dissolves and Remaps Barriers to Entry

The blurring of traditional industry boundaries is an inevitable force, and you cannot build or rebuild barriers fast enough to shut that force out:

Asset infrastructure is not a barrier to entry if it can be substituted by virtual assembly like Airbnb or encased in a data or services front-end value such as Kayak.

Financial capital is not a barrier to entry if a start-up can raise a million dollars in weeks on Indigogo or Kickstarter, scale up with VC funding, and then undertake an IPO.

Regulation is not a barrier to entry if e-cigarette makers can elude tobacco regulation and Bitcoin can evade currency regulation—at least until the companies involved are established forces.

Technology is not a barrier to entry if far superior digital products and services can be developed easily with sensors, microcontrollers, mobile apps, and cloud services.

Brand is not a barrier to entry if a fresh, attractive brand like Snapchat can establish itself quickly, virally, and globally via social media.

Your insight is not a barrier to entry if better data can be crowdsourced from smart products, social networks, and mobile apps to discover things you never knew about your own customers.

Your customers' "loyalty" is not a barrier to entry when they are offered superior products from designers who focus on user-centric design rather than product manager intuition.

Many of the traditional barriers to entry and bounding walls of your industry are set to become permeable because of digital, and this presents a structural remapping problem. Scenarios won't look the same twice, and therefore solutions won't arise from a single, cookie-cutter strategy. Leaders must create new thinking, culture, and competencies. These will help the organization preempt market space invaders and adapt as the disruptions compound.

Be Healthily Paranoid

A gradually rising fear of digital disruption is common among executives, but at some point one of them must initiate a conversation about the concern at the executive committee table. The authors have heard many stories about that first conversation. Usually, the initiator is relieved to find that others are starting to worry about the general risk of digital disruption too, without being able to say exactly where or how it might arise.

Should your level of concern about what might happen rise to the level of mild paranoia? We think so. If every company is a technology company, it makes sense to adopt some management ideas from that industry. Andy Grove, former CEO of Intel, once wrote a whole book titled *Only the Paranoid Survive*[16]—that sentiment is now applicable well beyond Silicon Valley.

Maurice Levy, CEO of Publicis, reflected that view: "There is a paranoia that we all need to have. It is the young start-up guy who will take my business and will put my company out of business. That is something we should be paranoid about."[17]

Be Prepared to Make "Techquisitions"

Maurice Levy's answer to fending off disruptive competitors was to acquire some of the tech-savvy capabilities his company needs.

"Techquisition" is our name for that strategy. In 2014, Publicis (a marketing and communications agency) acquired Sapient, which makes and sells an e-commerce technology platform—but Levy was after more than just the platform. He wanted that firm's capabilities to take his business into the new unclear ground at the intersection of three existing industries: marketing, technology, and management consulting.

"Why Sapient?" Levy said. "It is about the necessary changes to my business model. That is not only about communication or marketing. It is about consulting. It is about technology. So I can go to my client and say, 'I will help you to see what's coming in your business and I can help you understand and change how technology affects your business.'"[18]

The list of techquisition examples is growing quickly: Monsanto's acquisition of the Climate Corporation (a weather data science company), BBVA's acquisition of Simple (a digital bank), and Under Armour's acquisition of MapMyFitness, to name a few.[19]

Walmart has become one of the more advanced at systematic techquisitions; Walmart Labs has acquired fifteen companies since 2010.[20] Within the technology industry itself, there is a well-developed and long-standing ecosystem of start-ups being fed to large acquirers by VCs. For example, since the year 2000, IBM, Cisco, and Microsoft have each acquired more than one hundred firms. It's the way they have to operate, the only way to stay ahead when information and digital technology change so fast.

Your company may need to preempt invaders and make some techquisitions if there are technology-fuelled start-ups close to your space that could be part of a future winning formula. But be very selective. If you are in a mature industry it's likely your growth rate does not provide the cash to go wild with high-risk mergers and acquisitions. Only a few specialized tech firms will be directly relevant. Finally, there's the culture problem. Even with decades of handling experience, the big tech firms sometimes squash the very asset they purchased. Taking a high-tech firm into your stable needs to be done with a great deal of thoughtful care, or you risk accidentally crushing it. Your management time and attention are scarce and expensive, so buying two or three firms might work but buying twenty or thirty won't.

Techquisitions create new leadership challenges, such as convincing your investors to come with you on a journey toward a different risk and revenue model. Here's how Under Armour CEO Kevin Plank addressed that issue in public conversation: "We have the hardware with Armour39. People may wonder if we are getting away from our core with this acquisition [MapMyFitness] because it's software, but it's a long-term play in the space."[21]

Armour39 is a heart rate and activity monitoring digital chest strap device that Under Armour brought to market itself, already an unusual step for a clothing company. However, MapMyFitness, the first acquisition in the company's history, is a cloud-connected mobile app that records data related to fitness activities such as cycling and running.[22] Under Armour makes stretchy fabric sports clothing and Plank may realize that one day sensors will eventually be embedded in the material of the garments themselves. He is positioning his company to better control the whole package of digital and data utility to the customer before a competitor beats him to it. This boundary blurring creates an entirely new industry—maybe it's called digital fitness. Plank is quite clear why he's acting: "There is no reason we should just sit around and wait for Google to do this."[23]

So it appears that a sports clothing maker has bought a mobile app company to preempt competition with an online search engine company. That is boundary blurring at work.

Claim Your Stake in Your New Industry Platform

Under Armour's actions are a great example of platform awareness. Kevin Plank sees that the value is in the data that digital products generate—and in who can control access to our aggregated data and services from different sources. The "MapMy" app name stem has many variations—MapMyRide, hike, walk, and so on. It's not addressing a single activity category; it's a platform for potentially integrating all of them.

Simple digital product extensions without data and services are not enough, because once you expose data and services from your internal systems to other organizations there are questions of standards and integration. If every company makes a digital product with different apps and different communication protocols and different data structures and different data storage and access places in the cloud, customers simply won't buy in. Life will be way too clumsy, time-consuming, and complicated. However and wherever they arise, we will value integrated platforms highly. We all know this because we have used the leading examples personally: Apple for media, LinkedIn for careers, Amazon for retail. These end-to-end integrated, cloud-based platforms of control are springing up across the landscape of the newly blurred industries. Here, there is serious strategy thinking to be done.

In Dearborn, Michigan, Ford Motor Company CIO Marcy Klevorn is very aware that our societies may in the future engage in a lot more vehicle sharing, for many reasons. If that's going to happen, we will need platforms for the exchange of data between the vehicles and the various actors in the marketplace. These actors might include drivers, rental companies, insurers, servicing companies, and local government providers of roads and parking. One approach Ford is taking is a consortium-based platform called OpenXC, an open-source API for cars. The company kicked off open challenges, in seven cities around the world, that are leveraging the OpenXC platform. "This is going to take us to the next level, and we're inviting people to develop applications on those platforms in some focused efforts," said Marcy Klevorn.[24]

Ford isn't the only big engineering company thinking about its platform play. At GE, the Industrial Internet has at its heart a big platform called Predix. Bill Ruh explained the kind of value a platform can bring: "We are inventing common application elements and putting them into the platform, so that you end up with 80 percent of the work already done."[25] That's what software platforms provide—a common base. They avoid repetition of software creation and rework in those functions and algorithms that you want to nail in one place, perfectly, and then reuse endlessly.

Here's how GE CEO Jeffrey Immelt explained the wider significance of the Predix platform in the context of the value network of engineering partners and customers that GE wants to work with: "The more we can connect, monitor, and manage the world's machines, the more insight and visibility we can give our customers to reduce unplanned downtime and increase predictability. By opening up Predix to the world, companies of any size and in any industry can benefit from the investments GE has made by eliminating the barrier to entry."[26]

Immelt believes that GE has built a software platform with strong functional capabilities, and now the company wants other industrial firms to come and play on it. But why would GE want other companies to use its smart software and analytical algorithms to process their machine data? A software platform becomes more powerful the more people use it. As David Bartlett, CTO of GE Aviation, said, "Making [the platform] available externally will also allow our customers and business partners to write their own software and become more successful. We want Predix to become the Android or iOS of the machine world. We want it to become the language of the Industrial Internet."[27]

Bartlett's attitude is positive and progressive, and hopefully everybody gets value out of the platform, but there is also a little healthy paranoia behind GE's platform play. Ruh said it well: "Our biggest worry is if someone figures out how to manage a jet engine in a better way, which is a bit like when iTunes disrupted the music industry."[28]

The peril is clear. If you have the muscle to build an open industry platform you should do it. If you don't do it someone else will, taking more market control. The smartest companies think about how they can create digital information platforms or redefine platforms of the past to stay in control as their traditional industry boundaries blur and many new entrants come into the redefined space. In that conversation there's a word that comes up often, and that is word "open."

Be Open Everywhere

Like most governments of advanced nations, the U.K. government has found it hard to keep pace with digital change. The government wants people to go online, and it sees online activity as a vital form of economic progress. It encourages the telecommunications industry to provide bandwidth and it persuades small businesses to use the technology more. But the government's own traditional, ancient, and bureaucratic internal processes for managing change just haven't kept pace. So, gradually, the U.K. government's use of digital to provide services started to fall behind. IT projects of all kinds had a reputation for being expensive, slow, late, and, worst of all, not fit for purpose. One IT trade magazine even created a "pull out and keep" guide to the failures.[29] A radical new approach was needed, and in 2011 the government appointed Mike Bracken as digital director for the "cabinet office," the very heart of the U.K. executive branch of government.[30]

Bracken sees many layers of openness in the progressive new approach he's leading at the U.K. Government Digital Service (GDS). One example is the open data and open API strategy, which allows businesses and individuals outside government to access many government systems and data sets. But the whole opening-up process started as an outside–in conversation that led to the foundation of the GDS and to Bracken's appointment. Bracken says, "The GDS is one of four things that a report, called 'Revolution not Evolution,' said should happen to government. I was a contributor to that report, though I was at *The Guardian* [newspaper group] at the time. The report actually consisted of a series of open letters between Martha Lane Fox, the then digital champion, and Francis Maude, the minister for the cabinet office. The point is that it's a strategy from without, not from within. It didn't come from either a political realm earlier or from the civil service structure."

Bracken is changing the way government progresses with technology by taking an open approach to digital. He's there because government opened up enough to let an outsider in. He's driving open standards, using open data, and staying open to skills and ideas from everyone. The GDS uses all kinds of people—academics, independent coders, interns—to help, on the basis that the public good is a mission that's open to all, not restricted to a small coterie of large IT services companies.

The most powerful digital businesses will be massively open. They will create platforms on which many other organizations live, and they will create ecosystems in which new and reshaped industries are founded, evolved, and traded. This has been happening, in plain sight, for quite some time already. Tens of thousands of businesses operate on and through eBay, Amazon, and Google. However, there are even more powerful peer-to-peer models starting to flourish today, like Uber, Funding Circle, and Kickstarter. You need to take an open approach to succeed because you simply won't get a compelling set of resources to play unless you do.

That's the smart approach that Steve Perry uses at Visa because it helps to build the platform by feeding in new ideas and inventions:

> I think it's incumbent on the big brands, the big engines like Visa, to understand where the new technologies will exist and what we can use and leverage. I think we also have a parental aspect as a big company to support the new start-ups. I open my office to three or four of them a week. I probably talk to two or three a day. If they get past the first fifteen minutes with me, I bring them in. We have invested in two businesses. I work with them because they will change my attitude to digital. They will tell me stuff I haven't thought of. I'm taking a lot of intellectual skills from these start-ups. I'm using them to help me change my attitude to new inventions.[31]

As Perry implies, there's a less transactional aspect to openness. It's a philosophical shift, a preparedness to look at and learn from a wider environment that has become accessible to you because of the digital world. Nowhere is it more important to do the best possible learning than in the area of medicine, where narrow-mindedness and myopia can literally cost lives.

At Texas Health Resources, a network of hospitals and related health facilities in North Texas, chief medical information officer Luis Saldana reflected on the cultural shift he tries to accelerate by "being social, being present there on social networks, and also really taking a constant approach to learning and being very, very open that you're going to learn from other industries. . . . It's not all going to come from health care but that you may learn from other industries as well. We're in the world now where we'll learn from Amazon or Google rather than health care companies and things in the future."

In the end, most companies can only co-lead the building of a new industry platform with others. Few have the unilateral authority or the resources to foist a platform on everyone else. To collaborate successfully, they must get involved and take an open approach, because the blurring boundaries of old industries will eventually force change. Organizations that are too late to the digital party will have no gift to bring, and the door might be closed in their face.

Be a Step Ahead of Boundary Blurring

Boundary blurring is one of the three big change forces that should frame your thinking about the world. The effect of digital technologies is to blur the distinction between creating value in the tangible world of atoms and creating value out of the data that comes from sensing and controlling that tangible world. Once these arenas start blurring, the market space and core competencies that are used to play the game begin to change. Once new competencies and insights become primary, companies can more easily cross from one industry to invade another. Sometimes that crossover creates intersections that result in entirely new industry categories.

Large high-tech firms sometimes seize boundary-crossing opportunities; however, the new opportunities are often so radical and unlike what the incumbents have seen before that only outsiders are likely to test and see if the opportunity is real. Shoals of small start-ups are often the first catalysts of the biggest changes.

Actionable Takeaways

You need to be an outside–in visionary to be strong and effective as a digital business leader. Such leadership is essential if you are to succeed in a world where boundary blurring is at work at many levels.

Convince your organization that there is no safe, "business as usual" hiding place. Any and all kinds of barriers to entry can be breached by digital innovation in products, services, or business models.

Monitor potential invaders at blurred industry boundaries. Your best long-term defense is a state of hyperalertness to the changes, opportunities, and threats, and this awareness will help you capture and apply new ideas early.

Build your own set of digital-era boundary-blurring competencies. Position your organization to preempt or quickly follow protagonists that reshape or transgress borders. Chapter 7 will explore what some of those new competencies are and how to lead their development.

Create the capacity to pounce on key technology acquisitions. As digital goes to the core of products and services, every company will become a tech company to some extent. Techquisitions can help accelerate your organic digital capability building.

Refine your view of the emerging digital platform that will control your industry. Keep looking for the biggest contribution and measure of control you can win over that platform, or else it might grow up to control you. Strive to preemptively remap market space to your advantage.

Create a new culture of openness. Cultivate a complete acceptance that you cannot make the changes you need without outside help, and be open and attractive to people, companies, ideas, and services you may not know exist or realize you need.

PART II

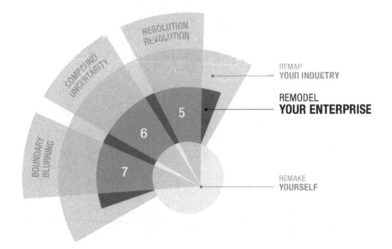

5

Digital Leadership Is a Team Sport

As digital technology penetrates into every product, the resolution
revolution will unfold. High-fidelity data of all kinds will let us
see new detail and assert precision control. This process will change
customer propositions, business models, industry models, financial
models, culture, regulation, talent, and more. For that reason, digital cannot be owned and executed as a single departmental function.
Every C-level executive will have her world changed. Every leader
must guide his group in making a significant contribution to the digital business endeavor. Most important of all, the leadership team must
act coherently in its digital pursuits.

Paddington, a small borough in the heart of London, has seen
industrial revolutions come and go. The great arches of its railway station were designed for the smoke of steam trains that no longer exist.
Its old canal, which once carried goods from the factories of the North
to markets in the city, now only brings pleasure boaters to trendy
waterside cafes.

Steve Perry's corner office at the modern headquarters of Visa
Europe has a panoramic view over this historic industrial landscape.
As chief digital officer, he knows that the waves of change ahead
could make conventional plastic credit cards look like the locomotives
and barges of the past. An advancing army of start-ups is harnessing

the power of the resolution revolution, applying mobile and cloud-enabled, real-time, and location-based precision to disrupt the payments universe.

"One has to look at it rather like staring out into the galaxy. Those millions of stars out there are the new start-up entities. They are entering my universe of payments where today we have a 60 percent market share across Europe. Digital is a transition from one new consumer proposition to the next. Digital eventually becomes part of the fabric of life. I do not think it's a phase, it's part of the evolution of money," Perry said.[1]

That recognition has led Perry and his CEO to redesign the way digital advancement is thought of and applied within their business. "In our past, we approached innovations such as digital wallet too much from a technology perspective," Perry said. "Today we recognize that the approach needs to be altered to focus on the consumer. It shouldn't therefore be IT-led, it should be event-led. What does the consumer want?"[2]

This shift in thinking has resulted in organization redesign. Nowadays, the work of technologists and business innovators is more closely interwoven than before. In late 2013, in conjunction with the appointment of a new CEO, this new thinking led to the creation of an end-to-end single digital entity at Visa. Perry said, "We think of it as an incubation process or conveyor belt for innovation focused on the digital space today. But there could be another disruptive force tomorrow. Really, it is a distinction in our organization between core and new propositions, one where my digital conveyor belt flows straight back into core."[3]

Two Modes Must Live in Harmony

Winning in digital business will be a team sport. While Steve Perry described a core business and a digital business, he explained to us that doesn't mean Visa created two separate entities. The two modes live in harmony. They use the same sales team and the same brand. Digital represents a transition, and innovations incubated in that mode eventually become core. Both modes are essential. Why must Visa take this approach? Wouldn't it be easier to create a separate innovative digital business entity and leave the old-style business intact? Perry explained the risk. "The Bank of England would call us in ten minutes if we are in danger of missing our settlement for the day. Serious U.K. default means that we are the Fort Knox of payment. We must be a solid tanker that doesn't sink. However, in my role my leadership style is schizophrenic. I've got to be 'corporate controls,' but in parallel I've got to innovate. I have to let entities come in and put them into an incubator and allow them to play with our systems but keep them away from the core system."[4] Payments must always be rock solid. Visa can't have a half-baked approach to digital innovation; it must be strongly linked into the core.

"We set up digital as an incubator," Perry added. "Once I prove that something works, once the child gets out of incubation, starts to almost toddle, it's no longer digital. You can pump it back into core. It becomes part of the fabric of what Visa is."[5]

That's the complexity of adding digital capability to an existing large-scale business. You cannot afford to let the massive, highly optimized operating machine become weakened or tarnished. Yet you must do digital innovation because it keeps the brand and customer value proposition fresh and healthy. If the executive team does not stick together to manage through the inevitable tension between those two modes, the company will cleave and neither part will be successful. And that issue is just as important in the business of burgers as it is in the business of payments.

Marketing matters a lot at McDonald's. In early 2015, the company appointed Steve Easterbrook as its CEO.[6] A year earlier, in his previous role as chief brand officer, Easterbrook had started important digital moves. He had hired an ex-Yahoo and Amazon digital leader, Atif Rafiq, as senior vice president and chief digital officer, and he had funded a new digital organization, with the role of spearheading how McDonald's will use digital and technology to grow customer experience and customer engagement. Part of the organization is based in San Francisco to place it closer to emerging ideas. The company used this team to capitalize on an opportunity to work as a launch partner for the Apple Pay service. Together Easterbrook, Rafiq, and CIO Jim Sappington convened a small team across their organizations to help the company launch Apple Pay in McDonald's in less than ten weeks.[7]

This new fast-paced direction dated to a 2013 "First-Look meeting" held in Oak Brook, Illinois, at which McDonald's conducted an early stage of its corporate strategic planning with the leaders of its twenty top countries and its senior executive team. "Digital" was the theme for an expanded meeting that year, starting with an outside–in customer view. McDonald's already had digital initiatives, but they were too disparate and fragmented across its global business. The executives decided that digital would become one of the key strategic cross-corporate initiatives to be addressed at a brand level.

Working from that strategic agenda, CIO Jim Sappington began assessing the leadership capability in his own IT organization. "When we did that, we determined we're very good at globally executing operations in a very complex environment. We're very good at large-scale technology deployment around the world," he said.[8]

But Sappington was also realistic that he had little or no experience with leading-edge digital engagement with consumers, in his own IT organization. This gap drove the McDonald's leadership team to search for a digital leader who could quickly build a team with solid digital experience. In October 2013, McDonald's hired Atif Rafiq to the newly created role of chief digital officer and Rob Gonda as VP global data and digital under Sappington in IT. Previously, Rafiq spent fifteen years in Silicon Valley at Amazon, Yahoo, and a venture-backed start-up he cofounded, and Gonda brought great digital and big data experience from Sapient. Rafiq reports directly to the CEO in McDonald's Oak Brook headquarters, relocating from San Francisco in order to ensure integration of digital efforts into the core business. He also spends significant time canvassing from ideas in San Francisco and major tech events like South by Southwest and CES in order to be "closer to the flow of ideas,"[9] as he puts it. Rafiq brings critical digital competencies, such as design thinking (see more in chapter 7), from his online business background. Rafiq and Sappington know that McDonald's requires highly integrated capabilities to drive relevant digital consumer engagement. They are aware that unless they work together very closely as a team, the consumer's experience will not be smooth and seamless.

"When you double-click on the experience of getting food from McDonald's, there's a whole host of things involved behind that customer journey. While it's very convenient, the definition of convenience is also changing and it becomes important to find opportunities to remove friction, streamline, and empower the customer at every step," Rafiq said. "This is where Jim and I have partnered to design and deliver the customer journey—infusing consumer technology like mobile interfaces or kiosks and new service models in the restaurant beyond current front counter and drive-through. It includes the entire customer experience—not just giving people a tool to create an order, but then how we actually fulfill it in the restaurant or in our drive-through."[10]

To deliver this type of integrated digital consumer experience requires close cooperation as Sappington explained, "Atif and I work very closely together. We understand the dynamics of the digital and the physical experience, how those have to fit together. By giving customers an added level of convenience, we also unlock a big business opportunity. Digital-based relationships with customers, and the data behind that, tied into our detailed restaurant information gives us a lot of insight that we don't have today. Making this come together will benefit our customers, and help grow our business in the process," Sappington said.[11]

Sappington and Rafiq are a model CIO and CDO pair, spearheading collaboration with the wider executive team to drive digital to the core of McDonald's. They understand that winning is a team sport.

Resolution Revolution Breaks Organizational Beliefs and Boundaries

As the resolution revolution progresses, more and richer data sources, each providing more granular levels of detail, become intertwined. New data often reveals awkward and contradictory insights that challenge deeply held assumptions and require substantial changes to the way organizations think. One such example arose at Babolat, when the tennis racquet engineers obtained data from their first connected racquets. They made an astonishing discovery—the sweet spot was not where it should be!

For years, racquet engineers had calculated the sweet spot on the racquet head using bench-testing tools and mathematical analysis. They then advised players where the ball should hit the head to get the best results. Players sometimes intuitively disagreed, but the engineers felt sure they knew where the sweet spot was because scientific instruments told them so. However, when the engineers obtained sensor data from the best players using the connected racquet on court, it showed the players consistently attained the best power from a different spot on the racquet. This was a shocking revelation.

CEO Eric Babolat explained how they then incorporated the *dynamic* nature of the racquet into the design based on the sensor data:

> The theory of the mathematics about calculating the sweet spot did not really integrate the movement that you make when you hit the ball—that changes the shape of the racquet head. So the sweet spot is not here, but it's there, or higher than expected. We started to design our first connected product with that in mind. It was obvious after a few months of play. That's just huge as information, because suddenly we realized…we, as in all manufacturers, were making an optimal place not at the place it was; it's just crazy![12]

New management insights like this, and the consequences they bring, often have no consideration, respect, or regard for man-made constructs such as organization silos. When leaders and their organizations gain this type of compelling insight, it changes their view on how to create the best designs for products and services. That, in turn, affects how the consumer wants to do business. These changes often span across old-model boundary lines, such as the stages of customer interaction that cross different sales and service channels. In a midsize business such as Babolat, any resulting adjustment to roles and responsibilities is usually quite easy to deal with. In a complex and very large global enterprise such as McDonald's or Visa, the leadership challenges can be herculean.

Resolving Tension Between Digital Change and Traditional Stability

Despite the best intentions of those in the C-suite, the transition to digital business will generate continual tension between digital change and traditional stability, between the new ways and the old ways. As Steve Perry at Visa pointed out, you need to design an organizational conveyor belt for digital innovation that flows straight back to the core. At Gartner we call this organizational design construct "bimodal."

The digital world demands greater dexterity to create value from technology, and a bimodal approach is vital to addressing that challenge. Your digital change resources operate in two distinct ways to meet enterprise demand: mode 1, a step-by-step approach that ensures efficiency and predictability; and mode 2, an agile, fast, and evolutionary approach.

In most pre-Internet-era enterprises, mode 1 has been made very strong. During the first decade of the twenty-first century, there was a great deal of emphasis on controlling costs and standardizing the use of information technology in organizations. It was a decade of systems consolidation, ERP standardization, shared services, outsourcing, and offshoring. These changes emphasized risk minimization and they caused a strengthening of methodical techniques of creating perfect business designs, project plans, and agreement before starting work on any kind of IT system. That became the dominant approach to technology—we call it mode 1. It is great for a low-risk, low-change, and steady-state situation. However it does not deal so well with Internet-powered market disruptive change and innovation. To do that, a more experimental and evolutionary "mode 2" capability started to evolve in the early 2000s, following the threat from the dot-coms and the rise of "e-business" in corporations. However, the financial crisis and great recession set its development back. Some of the biggest and most successful companies in the world now have to address the imbalance.

Headquartered in Milan, Italy, Luxottica Group is a leader in premium, luxury, and sports eyewear, with seven thousand optical and Sunglass Hut retail stores in North America, Europe, China and other Asia/Pacific countries, Latin America, and South Africa. The company also has a global wholesale network across 130 countries. In 2013, Luxottica Group posted net sales of 7.3 billion (U.S. $9.9 billion).

According to Group CIO Dario Scagliotti, CIOs and other technology and innovation leaders must have a split personality: a rigorous, detail-focused half and a creative, unstructured, and curious half. "The second half of the personality is about adapting," he explained. "As Darwin is supposed to have said, it is not the strongest that survives, but the most adaptable. This applies 100 percent to business, but the CIO's role in this is difficult."[13]

Focusing on people, Scagliotti has made his mode 2 organization flatter, with more individuals reporting to him. This not only puts him in direct contact with a greater number of talented people but also makes it easier to communicate the board's vision for change. "In the second mode, it is people who make the difference," said Scagliotti.

His team structure mimics the high-performance concept of elite military organizations or professional sports teams, where a single person leads a highly skilled group, with less concern about reporting relationships. "I wanted a high-performing team in which members are driven by mutual trust rather than organizational reporting lines," said Scagliotti. To keep a flat structure, he created several small teams—digital-to-consumer, digital-to-business, and digital-to-employee—without appointing a digital leader. The teams are independent but work very closely. In addition, Scagliotti brought new competencies in from the outside and recruited a diverse set of Luxottica people who possessed a great desire to succeed, inside knowledge of the company, and an ability to share business objectives. Scagliotti created that capability because Luxottica wanted to make the wholesale customer experience resemble what a consumer might have on eBay or Amazon.

The idea was, "Get everything you need from Luxottica—products and services—integrated on a single portal."

In the future, we can guess that Luxottica companies will need even more of this dynamic tech capability, because the company is making some of its products digital and connected. For example, the Oakley brand already sells smartphone-connected, augmented-reality ski goggles called Airwave.[14] In 2015, Luxottica CEO for product and operations Massimo Vian announced that the company continues to work with Google on a version of its "Glass" augmented-reality eyewear.[15]

To be successful in the digital business era, an enterprise must have the ability to harness new and emerging technologies and techniques to continuously improve or even reinvent its products and services. Technology is no longer a support function: it is core to product performance and customer satisfaction, and it must keep pace with the market. This is the organization's mode 2 capability.

Mode 1 operates like a marathon runner—in for the long haul; mode 2 operates like a sprinter—innovating in short bursts. However, the two development capability modes must be synchronized because the systems they create must operate seamlessly for the customer.

The mode 2 capability of older enterprises needs major expansion to keep apace of digital business progress. Sometimes, companies will transfer resources and funds from mode 1 to mode 2. In many cases, however, the mode 1 capability has been cost managed downward very intelligently for a number of years, and it does not have many resources to release. So for many business leaders, digital business requires a net new investment in the technology capability of the firm.

Every C-Level Leader Must Be Involved

The temptation to think of digital as distinct and separable into specialist enclaves is often very high. All organizations have a deep-seated bias toward perpetuating business as usual and repelling forces that try to change conventional and well-honed best practices. So let's spell out exactly why each and every leader must be involved.

The Board of Directors

The board of directors must revisit the core of the business, balancing the risks of action and inaction. The board ensures that the direction, purpose, and objectives of the enterprise are matched to the best interests of investors or other majority stakeholders, such as government. Modern boards are often highly attendant to managing risks, and digital presents plenty of those. However, the need to contain cyber threats is counterbalanced by the need to take decisive strategic action to avoid being made irrelevant by digital change.

Boards must steer a careful path, encouraging management to take sometimes radical entrepreneurial risks in new digital directions while not getting carried away by hype. Helping advise and decide what is "core" versus "noncore" will be a key supporting function of boards in the sometimes unbelievable world of digital change. Kenneth Daly, CEO of the National Association of Corporate Directors (NACD), sees it this way: "Today I think it is the rare board who doesn't consider [digital technology] in terms of being a disrupter. The strategy discussions that we have with boards almost always include where a digital technology is, where it's going, and how it fits in."[16] We will hear more from Daly on *how* to change the board in chapter 6.

The Chief Executive Officer

The CEO must shape the digital business vision—this work is just too important to delegate. Some previous waves of technology-enabled change have been delegable. Perhaps the COO could take charge of ERP, the CMO could take charge of digital marketing, or the CFO could take charge of business intelligence. Digital *business* change, however, can quickly alter the fundamentals of the business, including what customers want, what the product can be, what the industry is, and what the company structure and mission should be. These are matters that only the CEO can deal with, in conjunction with the board of directors, investors, executive team, customers, and other major stakeholders.

Leading from the front is essential. If the CEO does not own and drive the biggest and hardest decisions, then change will be superficial and weak. Digital business cannot be delegated, and it will not resolve itself.

David Duffy, CEO of AIB, shared that "the leader of the company needs to envision the future in terms of the risks. CEOs are primarily risk managers, and the risk of survival of your company should be at the top of the list. Leadership isn't battling against the technologists. Digital is just another input; if you, as a CEO, don't get it, then you've failed your company."[17]

The Chief Financial Officer

The company's CFO must adapt the financial model to the new cash flows that digital brings. Digital change is capable of utterly transforming the financial model of the firm, to the point that existing investors may need to transition out and new ones be brought in. For example, GE is developing massive new multibillion-dollar software and services business on top of business units that manufacture major capital equipment such as aero engines. Factors like the balance sheet structure, capital investment profile, free cash flow, revenue recognition timing, gross operating margins, and tax optimizing methods can change radically when digital disruption occurs. The thing you are monetizing and the way you do it will often change too, for example, from a product sale to a service subscription or an intellectual property licensing fee. Only the CFO can make these changes and judge how to time them.

The Chief Operating Officer

The COO will have to lead the transformation to new operating models, or perhaps change the nature of what he is operating. For a COO, many business model parameters are changed by digital. How do you make and serve the new digital product or service your customers are buying? What support services do customers expect? How do you provide those things efficiently and effectively?

Products might be dematerialized in part or entirely, or they might be substituted. New competencies will need to be incubated for 3D printing, cloud-based services, or digitally enabled products, and these new areas will need to find a home on the organizational chart. Existing areas will feel threatened, so dealing with active and passive resistance will become a key leadership issue for the COO.

Business Unit Leaders

Business unit leaders must maintain local continuity while contextualizing digital change. Educated and enlightened team behavior is essential within this group. BU leaders must adapt to change while carefully maintaining the traditional business revenues that fund the digital shift. These leaders must represent regional and local market issues fairly when the pace of digital change is uneven across customer segments. They are at the sharp end of selling new digitally enabled propositions to customers. If they compete against one another with different digital models or club together in an anti-digital cabal, precious months or even years can be wasted.

The Chief Marketing Officer

It is the CMO's task to accelerate digital marketing change without overreaching. Digital technologies, the resolution revolution, and an increase in precision and control are completely changing the way marketing is done, from big data customer analytics to mobile advertising. So the CMO must be intimately involved in the digital transition. However, we must also acknowledge another key fact: the CMO is *not* solely in charge of digital business. The CMO leads digital marketing. This is an area of confusion in many firms. Digital business will likely change your products, your business model, and your strategy, and may even redefine the industry you are in. Most CMOs do not have that much power and authority. CMOs are often highly persuasive C-leader personalities. Sometimes that permits others around the table to shirk responsibility in the face of apparent CMO "ownership." That could be a fatal mistake.

The Head of Sales

The head of sales must be prepared to adjust channels and the sales force. In the B2B world, the head of sales is often the person with the most customer-facing power and responsibility, usually more so than the CMO. The head of sales must transition the account-managing sales force to the reality of the digital world. That may mean revolutions in the customer value proposition, the distribution chain, the contracting process, the sales cycle, or the pricing model—or in all of these. Digital change will often require sales force reskilling or downsizing, and these changes can be difficult and painful to direct. Sidelining the sales leader could cause the whole endeavor to fail.

The Chief Human Resources Officer

The CHRO must build new talent pools, hiring methods, and career paths. When digital business change strikes, new competencies and new pieces of organization design are required, often urgently. Some of the talent the company needs is wholly unlike that it already has. Some may be so new, the talent must be sourced externally and some incubated internally—data scientists, for example. However, existing employees with deep industry knowledge also need to be retained and retrained, sometimes uncomfortably. Attracting new talent requires creativity in terms and conditions.

The shift may require carefully defining new cultural enclaves to protect unusual newcomers from corporate white corpuscles. Repeatable methods for dealing with strife and tension must be evolved.

The Chief Legal Counsel

The chief legal counsel must adapt to digital impacts on legal practice. Many industries depend on standard contracts, legal terms, and precedents in the judicial system. The customary enforcement of laws sets the boundaries of acceptable business practice. Optimizing the business on a day-to-day basis requires an intimate understanding of how to get the best results within this complex web of boundaries and parameters, but digital change can take a chainsaw to it all. For example, if an autonomous vehicle protects its passengers in an accident at the expense of a pedestrian it hits, who is liable for that "decision"— the passenger, the owner, or the manufacturer? Many complex legal scenarios will need to be tested and interpreted to evolve new policy.

The Chief Strategy Officer

The chief strategy officer must make digital a key part of corporate strategy. About a third of large companies have a C-level leader designated as head of strategy.[18] Many are occupied with conventional business growth maneuvers such as consolidating markets by M&A or seeking adjacencies. Sometimes they work on internal transformations. Either way, we believe the majority of strategy officers will be involved in shaping or responding to industry digital disruption. If the strategy officer's main task is to make the company "more digital," her role is very similar to that of a chief digital officer (see below).

The Head of Risk, Regulation, and Compliance

Executives designated as heads of risk, regulation, and compliance must advance and make safe new markets. Digital business creates new kinds of risk, often taking enterprises into grey areas where policy-makers and regulators are struggling to keep up. For example, should a company use DNA profiling data? Does it know where its traders are sourcing the mining machine data that informs their market models? Is a mobile app–controlled power saw a reasonable product innovation risk? The head of risk and compliance will sometimes work with the head of legal and regulatory, if that department exists in the company, to lobby for and develop new regulations that will be key to the development of new markets.

The Head of R&D

Whatever products your company makes or whatever services you provide, someone is leading the research and development of new and better offerings. That person will find that digital capabilities are changing the game in two ways: first, and most obvious, digital will embed itself into your innovations; second, and sometimes less obvious, digital capabilities can change R&D methods dramatically, perhaps leading to breakthroughs and acceleration. At Babolat, tennis engineers originally added sensors to a racquet so they could learn about it in the lab. Eventually, they put the sensors in the actual product so they could learn from match play. In arenas such as public health, big data analytics on massive open data sets could be a research game changer.

The Chief Information Officer

The CIO must integrate *all* the tech and the roles that touch it. Thus, the CIO will be one of the most important players in digital business leadership, and as time goes on we expect this role to be substantially redefined by digital. The era of focusing mostly on back-office systems and internal business administrative efficiency is fading into history. Today's CIO must be forward-looking, creative, and thoughtful about future business designs using all kinds of digital technology as a tool for customer-facing innovation. The CIO will become the integrator of the many kinds of digital change that the other C-suite leaders are trying to make. It will be a factoring role, concentrated on looking for the commonalities that can speed progress by simplification. This will involve orchestrating the creation of new systems and new competencies, but often these won't be owned and operated by IT.

The Chief Data Officer

The chief data officer must evolve, exploit, and control data as an asset. CDO is a new role that creates coherent policy control and ensures that data assets are exploited as the resolution revolution creates shocking new opportunities and threats. Mark Fields, CEO at Ford, told us, "At Ford, we believe customers own their data, and our role is to be trusted stewards of their data. We have appointed our first global chief data and analytics officer, who is helping us expand our approach to data use, gain greater insight into consumer behavior, and use it to speed up the pace of innovation throughout our business."[19] We will explain this role in greater detail in chapter 6.

The Chief Digital Officer

The chief digital officer will drive accelerated digital business change where needed. This new role has emerged over the past few years, and it has echoes of the "head of e-business" role that evolved between 1998 and 2005, as the first wave of Internet change impacted companies. Like that role, the chief digital officer is a strategic change agent, hired or elevated to accelerate digital quickly within the enterprise. We'll discuss this role more in chapter 6.

Leading a Team Beyond the Four Walls

Many of the digital leaders we interviewed for this book continually build and recombine teams of people from both inside and outside the organization to conquer a problem or achieve a goal. They will work with the R&D people from a technology mega-vendor at the same time that they hire a two-person specialist firm to draw on their mobile-app-user interface skills. They will contract with a small Chinese manufacturer on Alibaba to make a test run of a few hundred plastic cases, based on a shape they originally worked out with a local design firm and a 3D printer. They will open their doors to undergraduate software interns and makers for "hackathons."

Sometimes the role of the digital leader is more like that of a movie producer than that of a conventional corporate operations manager. He brings together many small, specialty, and independent or freelance resources alongside the mainstream full-time resources to create an outcome. Here are examples from the cases in this book:

• The Bharatiya Janata Party crowdsourced its highly successful 2014 election manifesto, and works with numerous start-up technology partners.

• Ford Motor Company is running a series of open mobility experiments with partners all over the world.

• Babolat partnered with a small company spun out from a French nuclear industry incubator to develop the sensors in its revolutionary racquet.

Who Orchestrates Taking Digital to the Core?

Digital business is a team sport requiring everyone's involvement. If any one member of the crew is not rowing in time, the team will surely lose. Marketing can't convince customers to buy old products that a generation of digitally savvy consumers doesn't want. R&D can't

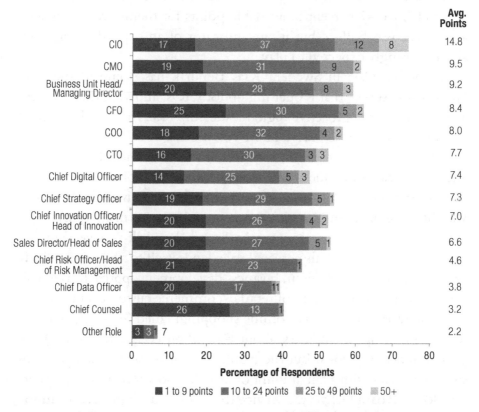

FIGURE 5.1 CEOs' Views of Who Leads Digital Innovation

beta test digital products that legal isn't ready to sign off on. Strategy can't progress if regulatory affairs can't win the regulator over to a new point of view. Sales can't confidently sell online services that IT can't quickly evolve and properly maintain. The CEO can't promise customers a bright new tomorrow if the team can't deliver, and the board can't convince investors to stay loyal if the company looks like it's on the victim list in the next wave of industry disruption.

But in any team there must be direction setting and pace making. In the Gartner 2014 CEO Survey,[20] we asked CEOs, "How will you distribute relative responsibility for leading digital innovation and change over the next two years?"

CEOs distributed the available points fairly evenly across the C-suite, viewing digital as a "team sport." We believe this reflects the growing realization among CEOs that every leader must become a digital leader. Also in 2014, we asked the same question of CIOs. They claimed 47 percent of available points for themselves. This self-assessment was bullish, but it's an indicator of an expanded role they are increasingly expected to play.

At Volvo Cars in Sweden, Klas Bendrik has occupied the new "permission space" that is opening up for CIOs, allowing them to play a bigger and more proactive digital leadership role. In 2012, he formed an innovation team to "drive IT in Volvo Cars."

"If you want innovation, the IT organization must be proactive, and be the leader in some areas," Bendrik said. "At Volvo, IT is responsible for the vehicle cloud (real-time data and connectivity) and the data warehousing of car information (storage and long-term analysis)."[21]

As a member of the innovation board, Bendrik is a very visible innovation leader, and his personal style lends itself to such digital leadership. Taking an outside–in, business development approach, Bendrik found that about 60 percent of retail e-commerce customers in Sweden had a delivery problem with online shopping: failed first-time deliveries were costing the industry about €1 billion (U.S. $1.3 billion) per year in redelivery costs. But the trunk of a car is a metal box that can store deliveries with a fair amount of security. So Volvo and its partners developed Roam Delivery, a service that required a high level of innovation, collaboration, and coordination both inside and outside Volvo.

Bendrik is working on many more such innovations. Those center-ing on long-term developments—autonomous vehicles, for example—are part of a highly structured, cross-functional, and well-funded innovation program led by vehicle R&D. An innovation board comes up with suggestions of its own, and development funds are provided by the various company functions.

Leadership in digital business must be an orchestrated capabil-ity. Every leader has to play a part, and there must be considerable synchronization from the whole team to deliver on the kind of digital product and service promise your customers expect you to make and keep.

Actionable Takeaways

Revisit what is core, balancing the risks of action and inaction. The resolution revolution and the product remastery it requires will challenge understanding of the company's role in the world. There is a risk of the company being made irrelevant if it does not act. Only the board of directors, including the CEO, can shift the fundamental purpose and direction of the firm, so change must start at the top level.

Involve every C-level leader, with no exceptions. Digital can't be a silo. Digital change is so deep and wide it impacts every business function. The CEO must be involved—digital's impact is too substan-tial to delegate. Each C-level leader around the top table has a clear and specific role to play. If anyone stays on the sidelines, she will hamper the whole team. In a highly disruptive environment, you can't afford to lose time by moving at the pace of the slowest.

Ensure that the entire team is tightly bound and working closely together. The resolution revolution will change customer needs, products, services, and fundamental beliefs about the business. That, in turn, must lead to the restructuring of areas and the redefin-ing of relationships. If you don't start with a clear understanding that digital is a team sport, you will squabble and fail.

Evolve the CIO role; CEOs need digital leadership, not passive service. Old-style CIOs, with their heads locked in back-office efficiency thinking, cannot drive the enterprise to the new customer- and product-centric world of digital. Sometimes new change agents will be brought in to redirect the way that technology-related leadership operates, the role it has in the firm, and the way it is perceived. Digital officers will be part of that. Eventually, the role of CIO will be redefined.

Create a bimodal capability harmonized across one team to resolve tension between digital change and traditional stability. There must be a pipeline from raw, new, high-risk digital innovation at the customer interface, through to solid, high-availability, day-to-day performance. An enterprise design that assumes occasional change that can be thrown over to a back-office-only IT function is no longer fit for purpose.

6

Upgrade to a Digitally Savvy C-Suite and Board

The compounding uncertainties arising from advances in digital technology coupled with customer, cultural, and regulatory change make possible new products and services, business models, and business strategies. However, if your leadership is locked into an old mindset it may not see, let alone act on, the opportunities or be aware of the vulnerabilities these changes create. As a leader of leaders, you must change their thinking patterns to put digital right into the DNA of the firm. That task might sound daunting, but as we will see with some specific examples, it is possible. Taking digital to the core entails remodeling the company at the board level and at the executive committee level, guiding your leaders on a digital journey that enables them to comprehend and embrace the full possibilities of digital business.

A massive gathering of people watched Narendra Modi, candidate for prime minister of India, take the stage for his rallying speech. His vibrant blue kurta looked crisp and neatly pressed as he greeted the audience. In a hundred other locations, audiences felt like they were seeing the same man. In 2014, Modi was digitally delivered to the multiple stages using 3D holographic volumetric projection technology. It allowed him to personally address many more voters across this vast country of 1.2 billion people in 3.2 billion square kilometers.[1]

According to Arvind Gupta, innovation evangelist and head of information and technology for the Bharatiya Janata Party (BJP), "In the forty-five days before the election, a candidate can typically attend and speak at a maximum of 180 rallies. However, using 3D holograms, a candidate can 'attend' two thousand or more rallies. Ours was the only party to deploy this technology. Digital is in the DNA."[2] That's the answer Gupta gave when asked why other political parties in India failed to take advantage of information technology that is equally available to all. The deep conviction that the use of technology could bring people together helped the BJP win an historic landslide in the world's largest democracy. A total of five hundred million people voted, of which two hundred million voted to elect Narendra Modi prime minister.[3]

"The party has a digital DNA because we were the first political party in India to launch a website, way back in 1998. It was way, way ahead of its time. Ever since, we've always used technology for communication, but also for governance," Gupta said. But to stay fresh and keep this attitude going, this belief must be refreshed. "In 2009 and '10 we identified the technology of the future and started getting people trained in those technologies and also evangelizing the use of those technologies within the party structure from top to bottom. We had great executive sponsorship—they said let them do their job."[4]

Gupta gave an example of the way his team experimented with the technology locally to build confidence and belief in using it later for the national election process: "In 2012 we started a crowdsourcing exercise for a state election, to collect input for the vision statement on our website and for the manifesto. We were surprised that we got more than 100,000 meaningful suggestions. Then we launched it in a much grander manner closer to the national election."[5]

Many of the political leaders in the top committees of the party are older people. Modi himself was sixty-three at the time of the election. We asked Gupta whether the average age of committee members made it difficult to create and sustain deep belief in a dependence on digital innovation for political campaigning. "Prime Minister Modi is, from a digital perspective, in his mid-thirties, I would say. The other leadership of the party kept their faith in the digital campaigns because they could see the results. Not everybody is at equal level of understanding but they said, 'Hey, this is producing results and it is an amplification step. It is not a step that is causing us to stop something else.'"

Gupta told us that the leadership could see that digital techniques had the highest return on investment among campaign methods. "They also understood that it marries with the demographic that is the new India...two-thirds of India was under forty at the time the elections came about. To communicate to a younger audience, you need to use modern technology as much as possible,"[6] he said.

In 2014 the BJP combined analytics, social media, the Internet, and mobile technology to produce personal communications and other messages that would reach the highest number of voters in a 360-degree manner. To reach these voters, the BJP used social media to mobilize ten million committed volunteers. Volunteers were organized online to cover as many voters as possible, and were supplied with big data information gleaned from social media and other sources. "The power of people is immense if you engage and empower them," said Gupta.[7]

The resulting voter turnout represented a 12 percent increase, including the highest-ever turnout of voters under forty, helping to win the election for Modi. "First-time voters were very enthusiastic," Gupta added. He also credited digital media with giving his organization leverage. "This didn't require 'gazillions' of people—my direct team is forty people, and half of them are volunteers. Our competitors lack the executive sponsorship that we have. We are led by passionate people who understand technology. We have always used technology but took it to a new level in this last election."

The organizations that are most advanced in changing themselves by taking digital to the core recognize that the top leadership must really believe it, and digital must become deeply ingrained in the culture. Gupta traces that conversion process back over more than a decade, to the first BJP websites. It is important to recognize the history of the journey and build upon it. That same deep, long transition has been going on inside GE.

Raghu Krishnamoorthy is VP of executive development and chief learning officer at GE. The very existence of his role says something about the way a company must think and design itself for deep change if it intends to survive at scale from decade to decade without getting disrupted. According to Krishnamoorthy, "About ten years ago, we created a course on leadership, innovation, and growth. We used to focus that on innovation marketing. Now, we're using the same format for digitization, for culture change."[8] He continues, "We are taking our senior executives to Singularity University in California, where we are able to see the future of the digital world and see what it means for us."

Singularity University, a teaching organization located in Silicon Valley, has as its aim "to educate, inspire, and empower leaders to apply exponential technologies to address humanity's grand challenges."[9] Founded in 2008, Singularity University provides specialized programs for corporate executives and government leaders. Providing this kind of education program is one way an organization can begin to willfully change itself from the top down—by creating a more digitally savvy C-suite and board. Krishnamoorthy points out that when GE hired Bill Ruh into the leadership team to create the GE software center, the company also gained an educator and mentor. "Bill is teaching us a lot about how we will be able to use the Internet as a multiplier and what that will look like for us," he said. "The fact that we now have capability within the organization to teach us and drive us in that direction is another important step we have taken over the last few years." It's part of a long-term program of learning and change.

In most companies executives are busy running the business, so taking time out of their schedules to redevelop them to requires some justification. Why is GE doing this now? According to Krishnamoorthy:

The digitization era is forcing us to go through an inflection point at a much faster rate than we have ever done before. The curve is starting to bend, and we need to make sure that the pace of change inside the organization matches, or in some cases is ahead of, the pace of change outside. Because otherwise, you will always play catch-up as opposed to leading the change. That's the biggest trigger we have experienced in terms of how the cultural anchors of this company need to echo the changes happening outside in the context.[10]

One reason the leadership team at GE empowered Krishnamoorthy to help rewire the way they think is that they knew they had to change top down if the next generation was to succeed. They commissioned a group of millennials, called the Global New Directions group, so they could understand the kind of organizational culture the company would need in the future. "They [the millennials] told us they were ready for a more horizontal, agile, 'connect and inspire' model as compared to the 'command and control' model the boomers are used to. We had to become more decentralized and simpler to do business with, and had to delegate power to where the action is," Krishnamoorthy wrote in a *Harvard Business Review* blog.[11]

You might be tempted to dismiss this piece of top-down management reengineering as too advanced for your organization. After all, GE has always had an unusually high reputation for meta-level thinking about and application of new management methods. However, this kind of deep change is being asked of CEOs by their boards. As Maurice Levy at Publicis said to us, "I know a lot of boards with people pushing the CEO to do more digital. Many times, I have received a call from a CEO saying, 'Maurice, I have a board meeting. My board is pushing me to do this, can you help me in that presentation?' This has dramatically changed."[12]

Every Leader Must Become a Digital Leader

Every leader must be a digital leader because every company is becoming a tech company—it is just a matter of degree. This change is occurring in response to the arrival and timing of the key tipping points in particular market spaces. Quicken Loans is a particularly useful example of achieving a digitally savvy culture early. Quicken Loans wasn't born on the web, but its predecessor firm was acquired during the dotcom boom years by Intuit, maker of the highly popular *TurboTax* and *QuickBooks* software. Since being bought back by its original founder in 2002, Quicken Loans has refocused solely on online lending and an Internet-era strategy.[13] Quicken Loans is now the second-biggest mortgage loan originator in the United States, closing $140 billion of mortgage volume in the United States in 2013–14.[14] It rated highest in the J.D. Power customer satisfaction survey for a fifth consecutive year, because of its technology-driven client service and partly by delivering industry-leading cycle times to close a new loan.[15]

Quicken's CIO, Linglong He, says Quicken Loans is "a technology company that does mortgages extremely well." She describes the mental model that Amazon used to digitally remaster the book industry and Netflix to remaster the video industry, and discusses how Quicken Loans is on a similar mission to digitize the loan process to deliver market-leading performance. To achieve this, Linglong He constantly compares herself and Quickens Loans' capabilities with those of core technology companies. She nurtures a digital culture that closely resembles those found in Silicon Valley, but it's actually in a very different place—downtown Detroit. You can do this anywhere; it's a mind-set, not a location.

Thinking of your company increasingly as a technology company and having a higher quotient of digital savvy is a fast-emerging pattern among leaders. Jeff Immelt, CEO of GE, has said, "We believe that every industrial company will become a software company."[16] Mike Bracken, head of digital for the U.K. government, has introduced "Digital by Default"[17] as a statement of the way services should be delivered. To lead other leaders on a journey toward a set of beliefs like these examples, the best place to start is at the very top of the organization.

Start with the Board

A 2014 Gartner survey of board directors found that a little more than half of boards were directly engaged in digital business initiatives. However, many still have limited or no engagement. So how can you change the attitude of a sleepy board that needs to wake up?

Ken Daly has spent his whole career working with and observing boards, early on as an audit partner and head of the risk management practice for KPMG, and more recently as CEO of the National

Association of Corporate Directors (NACD). He has testified before Congress on the impact of Dodd-Frank, and he is regularly called upon by the *Wall Street Journal,* the *New York Times,* and other media to provide insight on modern boardroom trends.[18] Daly sees several catalysts for a boardroom mood shift on digital. The first is cyber threats. "Cybersecurity certainly has everyone's attention. It has moved up at the full board level. I think there is not only a changed opinion, but it is now being taken up with some aggressiveness by boards," Daly said.[19]

Though security risks constitute a negative possibility rather than positive opportunity, they at least sound a wakeup call, so anyone trying to extend the board's conversation about digital business might start there. But security isn't just a corporate issue, according to Daly. "I think the tipping point has been that a lot of the directors themselves have been subject to phishing issues or other matters that have led to it being a very personal thing," he said. Security incidents—the threat to brand and reputation, and the corporate and personal consequences— prove key to getting directors to think harder about digital business. Consider helping directors with tailored personal advice on staying cyber-safe, then broaden the conversation.

Another key eye-opener for directors is their personal use of mobile devices and the way those get built into their lives and their family's lives. These devices can offer a great opportunity to influence. Daly noted, "The advent of everybody using iPhones and iPads in the director community means they can see that things in the everyday world are very digital." Consider the opportunity that gives you: those devices are a "channel" to the board. What content could you place in that channel to start influencing their thinking about digital?

Look at the Big Picture

Use small conversational opportunities—about the commercial success of their favorite smartphone apps such as Uber, for example—to expand to the big picture issues, such as what it means to operate in a world of digital uncertainty, how boundaries between industries are blurring, and how your products and core competencies might have to change. How do boards move beyond incremental discussions about cybersecurity and mobile apps to that more strategic level? Daly said that he thinks looking for the bigger opportunities in digital depends on the type of company:

> The key success factor is to have a company that, while it's still making lots of money and has lots of capital, actually takes wise opportunistic chances. General Electric does that. 3M does that. But there are companies that, for a lot of reasons, many of them political, are not able to do that. That's the Kodak story. The folks in charge of the traditional cash flow were unwilling to really let other organizations within the company grow up, they stifled growth. I think that's a great example of how you should *not* go about doing it.[20]

But who typically ignites the broad change of thinking in boardrooms, when it comes to digital? Daly said the catalytic leader often comes from outside the group: "Many times it is an innovator within the company. Or it could be a director who has a broad view of what's happening in the marketplace and can see a technology trend coming that has a likelihood of disrupting what the company is doing. I don't think it's the risk officers or the risk committees. It is the innovators and those who take the time to better recognize what's happening in the marketplace—and that could be anybody."

Perhaps you have been waiting for the risk committee to conclude that the risk of inaction—in the face of a possible Kodak-like disaster or Uber-like disruption—outweighs the risks of doing new things with digital. Daly suggested that scenario is unlikely. He believes an innovator will wake up the board, and that's often an outsider. It could be anybody and that means it could be *you*. In the end, that's what leadership is about—not waiting for someone else to make it happen.

Don't Educate—Make the Board "Aware"

Before you start telling a board what it should do, you need to be sure of your ground. It's too easy to have a narrow perspective when you see the world framed only through the window of your own company.

Daly had a solution to help with that issue as w[...]
that you speak to a buy-side analyst to understa[...]
about your company, what they think about the in[...]

Taking a broader outside–in viewpoint mal[...]
sense. To convey your ideas successfully, though, [...]
some very capable and experienced people who do.......ways appreciate being told they have missed something important! So how do you
teach them without seeming condescending? "Directors don't like to
be told they are being 'educated' but directors do like to be told they're
being 'made aware,'" Daly said. Describe what's going on out there—
developments in the marketplace, products, strategy, commerce—
focusing especially on news from outside your industry, because often
the disruptor comes from another arena. "Company management may
or may not see the freight train coming, so we recommend that the
board periodically bring in experts to talk about innovation, creativity,
and the disruptors they see out there, even if it's not specifically about
what you are doing."

Gathering the outside–in view and offering it as a way to gradually
raise board awareness is an obvious strategy for digital leaders to pursue. Of course, increasing board awareness is easier if you are a board
director yourself. If you have technology-related skills and insights, you
might volunteer to sit on another company's board as a non–executive
director, to gain the kind of credibility needed to influence your own
board. However you choose to approach your own board, one thing is
for sure—language matters.

Diversify Your Language with the Board

Effective communication is essential to winning over boards. "We
asked the director community, 'What is the number-one thing that
that would help you in this digital age?' and the answer was really
crystal clear: the language," Daly said, "they said, if we cannot communicate, we cannot learn."[22]

Vocabulary changes very quickly in the digital context, and it's all
too easy for directors to find themselves out of touch and their advi-
sors to find themselves unable to get a point across. You might think

...ing the name of the latest social website as a verb is cool, and ...haps it works with the marketing department, but you could easily lose the board. We forget how much digital jargon accumulates in our daily lexicon: "selfie," "additive manufacturing," "MVP," "reintermediation." The average U.S. board director is sixty-three years old,[23] and might not move in quite the same circles as you do. This brings up another issue boards must consider: diversity. A board that is universally pale, male, and stale might not deal well with the compound uncertainties of the digital age. However, digital savvy (or lack thereof) is not just an age thing. Daly said:

> I know thirty-five-year-olds who couldn't get out of their own way on these subjects. Conversely, I have a good friend who's on our board, who used to be the CEO of a major technology company—he's seventy-two and he understands all this stuff. I think one of the big issues is diversity but not identity diversity (gender, etcetera). I'm talking about *cognitive* diversity, people who have different life experiences, different education lanes, different swim lanes, they have much higher likelihood of doing what you're describing than the board that looks all the same. If you have a whole bunch of people who are bookbinders, there's very little likelihood they are going to recognize that the digitized encyclopedia is going to take over their business.[24]

Boards face a lot of the same issues that executive committees do. Cognitive diversity is a root cause solution to narrow thinking that some smart companies have already figured out.

Take Executives on a New-Era Behaviors Journey

One thing we noticed about the companies that navigate deep digital change well is that they usually set the change in the context of a longer-term sequence. At GE, Raghu Krishnamoorthy points out that in the 1990s Jack Welch compelled the company to focus on Six Sigma for operational excellence, and in the early 2000s he transitioned to a period in which the company was focused on innovation. Now GE is taking another step into digital and the Industrial Internet.[25] That step seems more natural and less challenging when set in a long-progression context.

Executive committees need that context setting. These executives make up the current operational management of the firm, but some of them may have come from outside and may not understand how the current culture came to be. Many of them will be far younger, on average, than members of the board (they are more likely to be forty-three than sixty-three). However, simply being younger doesn't make them inherently digitally savvy. To get where they are, they may have spent twenty-plus years climbing the ladder and conditioning themselves to business as usual. Being good at high-performance status quo operations has often been the hallmark of their personal success, and fitting in to the old business model may have become a habit.

You have probably seen photographs of a large company's leadership team beaming at you from the glossy double-page spread of a business magazine article or an annual financial report. Often, one of the first things you notice is how alike the executives look. Same age, same dress code, same stance. You can change the monoculture.

This is where the CHRO can play a key role. Some companies design cultural development programs to help their executives see the wider world and gain different perspectives. The program might involve travel, job rotation, education, workshops, customer partnering—any and all means to increase the range of understanding. An important aspect of more advanced programs is tackling unconscious bias—the cultural norms we have based on the society or subgroup we come from.

If your company is going to deal with the compound uncertainties that digital is creating in your markets, if your company is going to see and seize the triple tipping points, the executive team really must think outside–in.

Turning Executives Toward Digital

Sometimes you need executives to take on deep introspection exercises in order to change a hardened culture in which people come to work every day assuming that because the company has been around for more than a hundred years, it will automatically be around for another century. Let's break the change process down into three clear steps.

Job 1: Prompt the Team to Think Outside–In

Thinking outside–in might sound easy and obvious, but clearly it isn't. There are dozens of examples of large companies that lost control of their destiny because they failed to do enough outside–in thinking about digital change—Kodak,[26] Blockbuster,[27] and SkyMall,[28] along with a number of music companies and book publishers, come to mind. These businesses were incapable of seeing themselves the way others see them. As a result, when digital disruption became obvious to everyone else, and even when others were screaming "Look out!," they remained oblivious.

Time and again, when we interviewed digital leaders for this book, that same question came up: How can executives find ways of looking at things outside–in and have the humility and wisdom to listen and respond? Steve Perry at Visa found a way by meeting hundreds of FinTech start-ups. Atif Rafiq at McDonald's is looking outside–in by observing restaurant customers in one country and transferring that learning to other countries. Mike Bracken of the U.K.'s GDS is doing it by making citizen users as the central focus.

Job 2: Awaken the Team to Digital

Executive teams don't "get" digital overnight; that single killer Power-Point deck does not exist (in chapter 9 we'll discuss an interesting approach one executive used to wake up her team). Even teams that seem to get it slip backward and need regular reinvigoration. A significant amount of continuing education is needed (or "awareness raising," if they feel too senior to be taught). You cannot assume the peop. your C-suite magically absorb technology shifts, new business mouel ideas, and the emergence of whole new competencies. They are fully focused on their day jobs, and technology change often happens too rapidly for them to keep up.

Even some CIOs struggle to keep abreast of a sufficiently wide digital change horizon. But as we identified in chapter 5, the CIO is only one player in this endeavor—the whole team must be involved, from the head of compliance, who must interpret Europe's "right to be forgotten" mandate, to the facilities and real estate leader, who helps find and furnish a downtown digital R&D hub that's productive for makers and coders but elegant for customer visits.

The whole leadership team must be continuously reinspired and reeducated. Here's how to do it.[29]

• Bring in external speakers regularly to address your executive leadership meeting. Use technology and business book authors, along with tech-company C-level executives. Also call on junior people, such as twentysomethings working in tiny start-ups or sharp college undergraduates working on data science projects.

• Create a curriculum and delivery channel for technology business education. Work with HR and training to set goals at every level of the enterprise. Tailor topics and delivery styles for the various types of participants. Require C-suite members to introduce classes at the start and talk with participants at the end. This will get executives engaged in staff conversations that spark new ideas and change perspectives.

• Encourage C-suite leaders to participate in a technology executive education course, such as Singularity University. Or create a custom program with a business school at a university that has a strong technology reputation.

• Immerse leaders in digital ideas at technology-themed events, such as CES, *Wired* BizCon, TEDx, Web Summit, CeBIT, CEATEC Japan, or Gartner Symposium/ITxpo worldwide.

• Enroll your whole executive team in a short coding course—for example, at Codecademy or Decoded—so they can see how ideas become apps.

• If your company makes physical products, get executives playing with "maker" prototyping tools such as Arduino kits and consumer-grade 3D printers.

Job 3: Upgrade Talent

No matter how much work you do to energize, enlighten, and improve the existing executive team members, your efforts might not move the company far enough, fast enough. The terrifying pace of digital disruption can require an accelerated response.

As we mentioned in chapter 5, there are two new C-suite roles you might add in order to get moving more quickly. Let's take a look at the chief digital officer and the chief data officer in a little more detail. The two are neither the same nor interchangeable, though both are tapped by CEOs to help accelerate change. They are unlikely to be long-term top-level roles, though a version of the data officer may become enduring.

Digital Officer

There are two kinds of digital officers. The more common but less powerful type is a leader of digital marketing. This person focuses on digital media and customer interaction development—in particular, applying social, mobile, and e-commerce in conjunction and more aggressively than would otherwise be the case. Usually reporting to the chief marketing officer (CMO), this role imparts new techniques and energy to the marketing effort. In doing so, it sets demanding technology agendas for both the CMO and the CIO. For a while, those existing C-leaders must yield some agenda control, while the digital officer accelerates the development of the company's digital marketing capability.

The less common but more powerful kind of chief digital officer is a business strategist, who often reports to the CEO. This kind of leader will design deeper business model change or even core competency

change as the industry is revolutionized by new tecl
industries, the core product or service must now
signed. Such radical innovations as 3D-printed sh
cars require deep strategic change beyond the scope
most CMOs or CIOs.

Digital officers are sometimes found internally, like Steve Perry at
Visa, whom we met in chapter 5. However, most are hired from outside, like Atif Rafiq at McDonald's. These executives come in to shake
things up, may not intend to stay more than a few years, and have few
vested interests or political networks to defend. Digital officers are often
hired from big tech firms like Google and Amazon, but also from digital marketing agencies, tech consulting firms, and mobile telcos.

Chief Data Officer

The chief data officer is another new kind of C-level leader. These
CDOs are appointed to recognize information as a strategic asset. The
tipping point at which the role is created varies by industry because
some arenas, like banking, are more information-intense earlier than
others. But once products embedded with sensors start streaming data,
every company in every industry will have data mountains to manage.

In 2014, A. Charles Thomas was brought in from insurance company USAA as the first chief data officer for Wells Fargo. He described
the starting point for his role succinctly: "Our charter is to ensure that
the appropriate data are made available to drive our most pressing business decisions."[30] That internal sounding role is a common starting
point for data officers, but most move on quickly to encompass customer value. Thomas said:

> Our customers give us information all the time. If you look
> at people's transactions you know where they are, what they
> buy, where they spend their time. The question is, how do you
> pull all of that together in a way that respects privacy but at the
> same time puts us in a place where we're proactively antici-
> pating customer needs? They're saying, "Look, I gave all of
> this information when I applied for a credit card or for a mort-
> gage or an auto loan. I expect you to know me. Don't offer me

roducts I don't need. Make sure that my data are protected. Make sure that you know who I am when I walk into a store."[31]

The traditional CIO has responsibility for the information *systems*, but not the information that is contained within them. The CDO becomes a central organizer and custodian of the information itself. Chief data officers are often brought in initially to "play defense" by governing the data assets that are running out of control. Later, they progress to "playing offense" by introducing stronger data analytics, data science, and data monetization services.

Think Like a Demolition Expert to Level the Ground for Digital Change

We encourage you to take a comprehensive range of actions when trying to upgrade the digital awareness and capability of your board, C-suite, and senior management. Out-of-time corporate cultures can be like those 1970s tower blocks made of steel and concrete. If you want to demolish them you have to drill many holes, lay explosive charges, and set them off simultaneously.

In Figure 6.1 is a list of multiple changes that companies are making. We tested this list in the Gartner 2015 CEO Survey.[32] As you can see, some are being used by more than half of companies surveyed, while others are used by less than a quarter.

If you have tried to implement some of these changes and they haven't yet taken hold, keep going and apply the others. The discussion that takes place during these activities will cover a whole gamut of management beliefs and business capabilities that have been developed within tech-sector companies over the past two decades. We will explore these in the next chapter. Don't stop forcing those conversations until you can say, hand on heart, that you have a truly digitally savvy C-suite and board. Because momentous change is taking place outside your company, it's important to promote a great deal of change thinking internally. Without it, you will face an increasing and perilous gap into which high digital-capability competitors will leap.

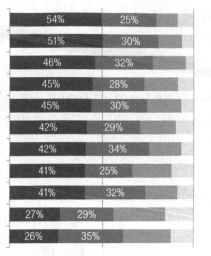

FIGURE 6.1 CEOs' Use of Various Methods to Increase the Digital Capabilities of Senior Management

Actionable Takeaways

Remodel your company—your goal is to make digital part of its DNA. Your company must become a tech company too, so you have to drive that thinking, belief set, and behavior right into the core of the firm. Digital thinking cannot be a veneer anymore.

Increase the digital savvy and cognitive diversity of your board. Because your company is subject to major external forces that could disrupt your entire industry, the board must be involved. An innovator who paints a big, multi-industry picture, taking the perspective of a financial analyst, can successfully change the board's point of view. Make board members aware (enlighten, don't preach), and explain in language they can understand.

Take your executive committee on a new behaviors journey. Your executive committee must be digitally remastered. Results like those India's BJP achieved with its election victory can't happen if half the leadership doesn't see the value of digital methods. Set your executives' journey in the longer, multi-era context so that it feels natural. Craft ways to help them see and change their own unconscious biases and see outside–in.

Expose the executive team to many digital stimuli to generate an awakening. Create a change program made up of multiple methods of stimulation and education to get them thinking about digital possibilities and customer necessities.

Upgrade the executive team with new talent, but do it sparingly. Adding one or two new heads who bring a lot of digital capability can help. Consider added a digital officer, data officer, or both. Frame roles not just in terms of what they will do but also what they will teach.

7

New Competencies Resolve Blurred Boundaries

To take digital to the core of your enterprise, you have to start bridging the gaps between where it is now and where it needs to be. You may need to get your company to cross the rapidly blurring boundary into a new industry. Information and technology need to become more like core capabilities of your enterprise and less like support services. You certainly need to add new digital competencies—and they have to fit somewhere on the organizational chart. You've got to span the blurring boundaries between existing departments and functions to make that integration work.

Some of the world's greatest companies know how to ride out trend shifts, crises, and even wars by passing hard-won insights from one generation of management to the next. Around 2010, while most businesses were still firefighting the global financial crisis, at 120-year-old General Electric Corporation, CEO Jeffrey Immelt and CTO Mark Little were already looking beyond the crisis. Scanning the future horizon, they could see massive digital change coming to many industries, including their own.

Immelt and Little looked at the tech sector and realized that if a competitor invaded with the right knowledge, it could disrupt GE unless they acted. However, because of their industrial domain knowledge, they knew that the company had a unique opportunity to lead in the digital space. But they needed a new level of advanced software and analytics competency. They recruited Bill Ruh from Cisco to become vice president of GE Software, tasking him with driving the rapid creation of a massive new software and data analytics headquarters in the heart of Silicon Valley.

Ruh's mission is to create a new core competency and change the culture of GE. In essence, he needs the company to accept that the kind of information technology Google or Facebook does is just as important as the physical engineering of rotating machinery. "In many ways, we are driving a culture change in the company, and we are totally rethinking the structure and organization, we're totally rethinking the processes," Ruh said.[1] "For example, we are driving agile development and extreme programming into the model. This is really a foundational shift. Our biggest challenge is that we've had to retool, we've had to get our people thinking differently."

At GE, software and analytics are no longer supporting functions; they have become core to the products and services, and thus they *are* the business. This shift of emphasis isn't unusual—it's becoming increasingly common.

At the U.K. Government Digital Service, Mike Bracken, executive director of digital and chief data officer, has led a similar transformation to take digital to the core of what his government provides for citizens. "It's not about fixing the rusty trains of public administration," he said. "It's about building some new ones using digital skills from the very outset.... Probably the best example of that would be at the end of the last session of the last day in Parliament in July 2011. The then Speaker of the House of Commons promised that when they met again, they would have an e-petition service so that everyone could petition the government...which is a [citizen's] legal right. It was a lovely throwaway line—then he went off on his holidays."[2] Such a challenge would have easily defeated the old IT capabilities of the British government's civil service departments. Not this time. Bracken said, "We created that service in six weeks with eight people for less than £100,000...What the GOV.UK platform says is 'We recognize you live in a digital world, you want something of the government, whether you're an individual or a business. Ask and you shall get that, whether it's information or a transaction.'"

To achieve this rapid digital delivery of services, Bracken had to push against the traditional thinking of other leaders in the organization. "Too many are still trapped, saying, 'Digital, that's like IT. We go outside to a big company and they do it for us,'" he shared. "I say, 'No, it's core, it's business.' For example, millions of people have signed up to register to vote with a digital transaction that we created. That's something I'm quite proud of because it's been done by twelve people who are sitting six floors below us right now. That anecdote alone tells you that we don't need a massive IT contract to change what is arguably the most important democratic service we offer: representation."[3]

Rebuild Technology As a Renewed Core Competency

"IT Doesn't Matter" was a popular article written by Nicholas Carr and published by *Harvard Business Review* in 2003.[4] Its premise that IT was a commodity, not a source of competitive advantage, influenced board-level thinking for a decade. However, after the financial crisis and great recession, business leaders reevaluated the idea that information technology is unimportant. In fact, it turns out to be highly disruptive. In the first fifteen years of the twenty-first century, massive new technology-fueled behemoths—such as Amazon, Google, and Facebook—arose at incredible speed. These companies now reshape industries such as book publishing, retailing, and automotive with their disruptive innovation. Though each is operating in a different sphere, they all exploit the same information technology power under the hood: Moore's law.

Faced with this reality, leaders in many industries are now scrambling to harness the same power for themselves and apply digital innovation directly to their businesses as a source of innovation for competitive differentiation. Gartner's 2015 CEO Survey[5] found that growth was the top business priority, and technology-related issues were second.[6] This was the most prominent position technology had held in the minds of

CEOs since 1999. By 2015, it had become a growth tool of choice, and when respondents mentioned technology, more than half used words associated with the modern digital era such as mobile, cloud, social, big data, or the Internet of Things. As the majority of CEOs started to move in the same direction around the same time, it was inevitable that they would contend with one another for the same customers and resources, using various digital business ideas.

Much of the conventional IT is still needed. However, a whole new collection of exploratory capabilities is now required to help innovate and set an agenda for the use of technology in changing business. In some ways, we are trying to revert to the position corporate technologists last held in the 1980s; the first few generations of CIOs were corporate technologists whose task was to revolutionize business models, not just make them more efficient. They innovated business directly through the application of technology in an entrepreneurial way. For example, a 1986 *Businessweek* article quoted Max Hopper, the CIO of American Airlines, as saying, "Our technology is a key part of our ability to expand," mentioning the in-house-developed SABRE system that created 28 percent of profits.[7] SABRE was an acronym for "semi-automated business research environment," a statement of its innovative exploratory purpose.

We are seeing a renaissance of that style of leadership, focused on an entrepreneurial spirit and competitively differentiating technology. To do the trailblazing today, however, you need a different tool set. GE's Bill Ruh sketched out a list for us. "I think today you've got to have cloud and mobility, and I don't separate those out. You've got to have a competence in cybersecurity. You've got to have competence in analytics and data science. Then you've got to have competence in your user experience," Ruh said.[8] "The hard part is that these groups see themselves as the center of the universe, so you've got to be able to bring them together in a way that they work together well. You've got to be able to get them to work as a team. Now, that may not sound like much of a competence, but it is."[9]

Ruh's colleague Raghu Krishnamoorthy, chief learning officer at GE, has been developing something called "FastWorks." It's a framework for entrepreneurs inside the company that helps them coherently learn and apply many of the techniques that Silicon Valley start-ups use. We'll share more about this in chapter 9.

Internal Boundary Spanning

At Spain-based global bank BBVA, CEO and chairman Francisco González has said, "There is no option but being digital,"[10] and he has reorganized the top team and injected new senior talent at the bank to make that happen. For example, the bank has a senior EVP of business development and digital transformation, a senior EVP of new digital businesses, a head of open innovation, and a digitally savvy head of internal ventures. Leading one of those internal ventures is Marco Bressan, chairman and CEO at BBVA Data & Analytics, one of several bank executives developing major new competencies for the company's transition to the digital banking age. He was very clear about the fluidity these new capabilities require of the organization: "I think this is a huge transition in companies that have traditionally had a hard and tall wall between business and technology. This wall cannot afford to exist anymore. Everybody needs to speak, be fluent in both languages. This is important."[11]

We have said that every company is becoming a technology company. To add to that, we can also say that every business unit is becoming a technology start-up. To achieve that goal, a range of new competencies is needed, but these can incubate in different parts of the enterprise and then extend their reach. There won't be a single locus of control because digital isn't a department—it's something that all employees are involved with, whether their job is writing words, hiring people, or managing money—digital capabilities eventually become common within most parts of the business.

You Must Be on the Same Playing Field

Your company, and many others in your industry, are facing a future in which digital technologies will become integral parts of your products and services—not just in the marketing of them. If you don't make that happen, someone else will. Your ability to differentiate will depend on digital capabilities that must fast become parts of your core competencies. You cannot just "source" this stuff—it will need to be part of your firm's DNA.

Maybe you start the battle with some advantages, like brand, scale, regulatory competency, or trading relationships. However, your opponents will often be "born-digital" technology upstarts. They are coming out of their zone and toward yours with many tools and techniques that have been developed and honed in Silicon Valley over a couple of decades. These are the methods that help tech companies succeed. You can't win against them by saying you are playing some old game in an entirely different space. They are coming for you. You must play against them on the same field, using the techniques of the digital business game.

You might find this field daunting and wonder how you can take your organization to this new place. Your task will be to sort the enduring competencies of value to your company from those that are

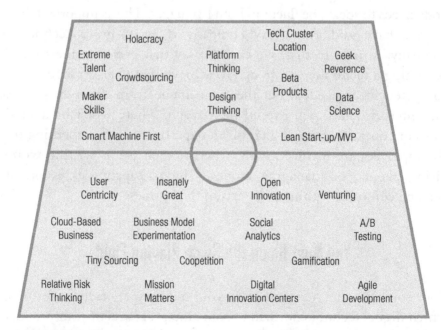

FIGURE 7.1 You Must Compete on the Same Digital Business Playing Field

either relative fads or relevant only to others. That will be a journey of courage and strength in your personal leadership.

Your task as a leader will be to create the understanding and the conditions that enable your organization to see the need to develop these capabilities. (In chapter 9 we will help you think about the clarifying and educating roles you must play, and in chapter 10 we will explain how you must attract new talent to help seed these new capabilities but also to map and define how they play inside and outside your remodeled organization.)

Develop New Competencies and Techniques

Figure 7.1 shows how different the new playing field is for digital business. Many of the cultural beliefs, innovation methods, and technical competencies listed are operating in born-digital companies—they're not "nice to have" options. It's a big list. We will explore a few key competencies in the remainder of this chapter; a quick explanation of the others can be found in the appendix. Your task as a leader is to decide which ones are relevant and to add them to your organization. This book is about leadership rather than detailed management, so it's beyond our scope to delve into the specifics of developing each one, but several high-level considerations follow.

Build or "Buy"

You can incubate a new competency from scratch by retraining and redeploying existing resources. When Shell started its technical and competitive IT group, employees were transferred in from the research side of the traditional IT department and also from the petroleum engineering parts of the company. Another way forward is to hire one or two key leaders as seeds for the new competencies—McDonald's hiring of Atif Rafiq from Amazon is a good example of that strategy. At Estée Lauder, CIO Denise Clark has been taking this approach to help accelerate the company's digital journey. "Hire really good people. I can't overemphasize that," she said. "We want to leapfrog some of the technologies of the past. They have to be innovative people so I can help the business create competitive advantage and bring that technology innovation into the company. I rely quite heavily on some of the new talent I've brought into the organization to help me do that."[12]

We also see companies "acqui-hiring"—buying a company to acquire its talent rather than only its product and customer base. Robin Thurston was the CEO of MapMyFitness, an app and online property that was acquired by Under Armour. Now he is Under Armour's chief digital officer, creating its connected fitness platform at a new digital headquarters.[13]

Separate or Integrate

New competencies can challenge the status quo, and may need protection while they develop. You can choose to place them under an existing head on the organizational chart, or you can choose to give them separation. As digital permeates to the core of the business, care should be taken not to create new silos. In 2014, McDonald's opened a new digital research and innovation center in San Francisco, close to the center of digital skills and culture but ensured that this new entity had tight integration with its Oak Brook, Illinois, organizational heart. Sometimes the competency may reside inside a business unit that then provides services to others, as Bill Ruh's software center does at GE.

At BBVA, Marco Bressan's team delivers services using a hybrid model: "We are an independent subsidiary, but not a P&L or a cost center. We're something in the middle. At the beginning of the year, we're a cost center. When we make new products, it's pretty much as a cost center. But as we deliver those products to the different business groups, they assume the costs. At the end of the year, the whole balance looks very much like one of our P&Ls."

For this book, we interviewed more than thirty-five leaders who are driving new competencies deeply into the core of their enterprises, often revolutionizing the organizational structure as they do so. A few specific competencies came up again and again, so we will explain a little more about them, starting with the one Marco Bressan is creating for BBVA.[14]

Analytics and Data Science

Earlier, we told you about the resolution revolution, the explosion of ever more detailed data that permits organizations to see what is going on with greater fidelity and to exercise ever more precise control. However, the sheer volume and complexity of the data simply overwhelms human capacity to do anything meaningful with it. You could have a team of analysts the size of the U.S. Army, but without tools they simply wouldn't be able to process the exabytes or even zettabytes of data available to you. A new kind of science with new kinds of tools is evolving to deal with the problem.

Data scientists use a wide variety of mathematical and algorithmic techniques to combine and analyze data from disparate sources and discover insights into which business decision—from the biggest to the most minute—can be made. They apply old techniques like time series analysis, but on a new industrialized scale on vast data sets that accumulate from all the activity taking place in the cloud. They also apply new techniques like data deep-learning neural network algorithms or 3D data visualizations. Importantly, they usually take an open approach, sourcing the tools widely but also sourcing data widely, often from outside the enterprise.

At BBVA, Marco Bressan has built a major team of data scientists to take the bank into what we might call the digital age, but he has a different point of view on that:

> Data is the substance, and digital is a place. One of the main trends that fuels the work we do around data is the process that I call datafication. Datafication is the incremental journey of real-world entities from the physical, analog world into the digital world. The process started with text and numbers and then moved on to increasingly complex things like music, video, and, right now, DNA, 3D objects, and so forth. The substance with which this is built, these tiny bits of information, is the data. We think about what we can do with that data, once they're there.

Who are the data scientists? The term data science is a new one, and there are few university courses around the world offering this specialty as a degree. This is a common problem for digital leaders—a lack of talent supply means they have to create a start-up for a new competency by blending a diverse range of people into a new learning-by-doing environment. Bressan continued:

> The emerging profession doing this work is about three years old. A data scientist is partly a computer scientist and partly a businessperson. You will find them at intersections; for example, somebody who studied computer science but had an eye for statistics; somebody who studied mathematics but liked developing or physics. When you start building your team, each of these individual people brings something into the game. We have people who come from the social sciences and people who come from engineering. Typically they are postgraduate. We have multiple PhDs.[15]

Composing such high-capability teams of people from disparate backgrounds is not easy. The leader has to create a culture of tolerance, respect, and mutual appreciation. "I myself need to speak the same language of the people I'm trying to bring to work with me and to collaborate with. Otherwise, they wouldn't come," Bressan said.

User Centricity and Design Thinking

There is one critical new capability that we encountered again and again when researching this book: user-centric design. It's something that accelerates digital progress. Digitally savvy leaders allow a small group of designers and developers to focus almost totally on the needs of the end user, whoever that is. All subjective internal voices and secondhand opinions are assessed against these objective techniques. Ideas and features are tested only by users, and only those tests determine the direction of advancement. This principle is something that Atif Rafiq was quick to instill at McDonald's when he joined the company as chief digital officer:

Design-led thinking leads to your user experience. It begins with exploration of a strong signal you hear from customers or intuition, which is an important ingredient—for innovators to have a strong customer intuition. It's important to use design as a way to paint the picture for what the opportunity is and what that experience could be. At the end of the day, it's the usability of your product, how people interact with it, that's important. It could be very small things around how many steps are involved or how clear a button is, color schemes, visual design—all those things. We pay a lot of attention to detail. Design is a critical ingredient at every stage of the process, and it's like this three-legged stool between the technical know-how, the design thinking, and then an area we refer to as "product management," which is always bringing the lens of the customer so that we ask the right questions about making sure it's solving a problem, a clear problem, and it's helping the user meet the need.[16]

At the U.K. Government Digital Service, Russell Davies, director of strategy, said that design thinking is at the center of everything. The GDS is making rapidly accelerated progress by focusing almost entirely on the user—the citizen—rather than anyone else in government, as a guide for what needs to be done and how it should work. Davies said:

Start with needs. Our number one decision-making tool is user needs that help someone to make it [the government online service] better. When internal people say, "I want this to happen. I want that to happen," we say, "Does that make life easier for the users? If not, we won't do it." For example: we had a massive fight with departments who wanted us to put social sharing buttons on every bit of content. They said, "There should be a Twitter button and a Facebook button and a LinkedIn button because people will want to share content and it will be easier." We argued long and hard about it. In the end, we did a trial. We put some sharing buttons on some content. No one ever used any of them. We said to the departments, "Look, no one's using them," and they went, "Okay, yeah, you're right."

In the old world, that would have just been an ongoing argument. Now, we're in a world where you can try things and see what happens. You can try a thing in the space of an hour. If it doesn't work, you can undo it. That's a big difference.[17]

Many of the other companies we interviewed for this book are keenly applying user-centric design thinking, including Zappos, Tory Burch, and Babolat. Most people know that user-centric design thinking is what helped make Apple's products "insanely great," as Steve Jobs would say. It would be easy to think that this capability is for consumer business, but it turns out to be universally valuable, even if you make big machines like airplane engines for other businesses.

Maker Skills and Building Digital Things

In the seemingly endless flat green farming country forty miles outside Paris, clusters of modern buildings poke out of the fields next to a tiny provincial airport. The facilities belong to Snecma (Safran), once a French acronym that translated to "National Company for the Design and Construction of Aviation Engines." Now Snecma is part of the $16 billion Safran Group of aerospace defense and security companies. If you are invited to visit the small facility called the Fab Lab you are ushered into a drab business meeting room that at first doesn't seem to match its exciting name. The lab's director, Fabrice Poussiere, explained what the facility does: "We use 3D printers, vinyl printers, cutting tools, and programmable electronic prototyping platforms such as Arduino, Raspberry Pi, as well as Lego, graphics, and multimedia, to move faster toward the storyboards we have already developed. We have a team of user experience (UX) designers, data engineer, IT engineer, UX researcher, community manager, and business developers."[18] Using this capability, the Fab Lab supported the work of an engineer who developed SFCO2 ®, a service to reduce airlines' fuel consumption by 3 percent to 5 percent per year, by analyzing engine data.

The meeting room was disappointingly dull until Poussiere reached for a small, partially hidden button on the wall. "Okay, now we have decided we like you and trust you a little—you can see the Fab Lab."

He pressed the button and a wall disappeared. One wall of the meeting room was made of smart glass that can switch from opaque to transparent—and through that glass is the lab full of wonders.

The term "Fab Lab" is not unique to Snecma—it is drawn from the word "fabber," a term used to popularize the idea of small-scale 3D printing by a Cornell University open source hardware project started in 2006 called Fab@Home. In this kind of lab, new Internet-connected digital things are invented. The multitalented people who work in them are sometimes referred to as "makers" because of the craft-like skills they possess, which they call on to make early working versions and prototypes of future products. Using easily reprogrammable microelectronics and sensors for the technical parts and 3D printers to make the plastic shell parts, these specialists hack, change, enhance, and combine existing electronic objects or simply invent new ones. But Snecma makes aircraft engines, the kind you find on a single-aisle Airbus A320 or Boeing 737. Poussiere's team isn't hacking those! Instead, these makers are working on prototypes of new diagnostic machines to help engineers find and fix faults.

This kind of digital prototyping and design facility is a new and important area in digital business. It is similar to what happens within Babolat's tennis racket engineering workshop. Once you have good working prototypes, you need to scale up. That means working with firms that can help build electronic designs and then work with contract manufacturers. There's safety certification, electronic waste recycling regulation, and many other specialist subskills involved in making digital and electronics products. However, you can't evade this inexorable digital direction. Technology will be embedded in everything. So best get started building your firm's capability.

New Business Cultural Capabilities and Beliefs

New technical competencies will be a major investment that help take your firm in a digital direction. However, these are just tools. A leader who wishes to take digital to the core must ensure the tools are applied. For that to happen, the management of the organization needs to absorb new culture, mind-sets, capabilities, and beliefs. It is only with these that you can span the boundary lines between old and new organizational structures, old and new business models, and old and new products and industries.

Platform Thinking

At every level, platforms matter. Industry platforms control how companies collaborate through ecosystems. Product platforms enable versions and variant of products to share some common core functions. Platform thinking is a characteristic of some of the most powerful technology companies today. iTunes is a platform for music. eBay is a platform for small and micro businesses. LinkedIn is a platform for the recruitment industry. In another example, Google's subsidiary company Nest started by making smart home thermostats and fire alarms but very quickly reasoned that its devices could become connecting hubs for all manner of digitally enabled home appliances. It can't hope to dominate all of those markets, so instead it is creating standards and a platform for others to join, called "Works with Nest." Osram, Whirlpool, LG, and others quickly signed up.

A company that is digital to the core is always thinking about, building, extending, and strengthening its own platforms and those it participates in as part of its management DNA. Often, it will also be looking for ways to undermine the hostile and controlling platforms of others. Like any other subject in this chapter, platforms could warrant a book of their own. It has become enough of a management discipline in its own right to be taught at universities; MIT offers a regular course on platform strategy, for example.

Brand-Safe Beta Experimentation

For many years, the "born-digital" companies like Google have placed beta (end user) testing versions of new digital services in the public domain. Many people come to rely on valuable but imperfect services that the provider is still fine-tuning. This technique is often vital to accelerate market feedback cycles and new product evolution. However this practice is not so easy for an established traditional major company to use. Dare you risk your precious brand reputation, releasing half-baked mobile apps that carry your multibillion-dollar logo? What if they go wrong? Sometimes the industry regulator will scrutinize and enforce perfection in financial services companies or utilities, in a way it would not do for adjacent start-ups. This is a delicate competitive disadvantage companies don't always like to talk about, but there are ways around it, for example:

- Using the employee base as a consumer test population
- Using a semi-detached sub-brand or white-label site as a safe place to test ideas
- Silently testing a new or different version with a subset of the total customer base

Relative Risk Thinking

Enterprises that are digital to the core do not dither. They take active and often substantial risks with digital technology to win and maintain their position in markets. This point of view is in stark contrast to the default thinking about the use of technology that has become entrenched in companies that see IT as a supporting tool rather than a core competency. There is simple but crucial logic required to sustain a truly digital company, and everyone in the executive team must learn to accept it.

- Once your product or service becomes substantially digital, its features, functions, and customer value are subject to exponential progress on the order of Moore's law.
- If you don't take the next digital innovation opportunity, someone else will.
- Because exponential progress creates large gaps between products very quickly, falling behind means you may not catch up.
- Risk is relative. The risk of *inaction* is high, and must be balanced against the perceived risk of action.

We know the danger of inaction within the tech sector because we have all observed the sudden sharp declines of once massively powerful and successful tech companies such as Nokia and BlackBerry. In the words of Mark Zuckerberg, founder and CEO of Facebook, "The biggest risk is not taking any risk.... In a world that is changing really quickly, the only strategy that is going to fail is not taking risks."[19]

Actionable Takeaways

Assume that boundary blurring will expose weaknesses in your digital capability. Industry boundary blurring will happen, and tech-savvy invaders will rush in. Digital is becoming part of your products and services.

Start to rebuild technology as a core competency. The old service provider/order taker, minimum cost, no-risk IT department model was simply not designed to help you invent better digital products and customer propositions.

Decide to play on the same playing field as your new competitors. You can't hope to win against tech-savvy digital greenfield competition without adopting many of the same behaviors and developing the same skills.

Champion the development of multiple new digital capabilities. Find the spaces to incubate them and help them span old boundaries on the organizational chart.

Evangelize digital management cultural beliefs. Even with the right skills on hand, you can't play to win unless you change the mindset of those at the top of the firm. Digital thinking is the new normal.

PART III

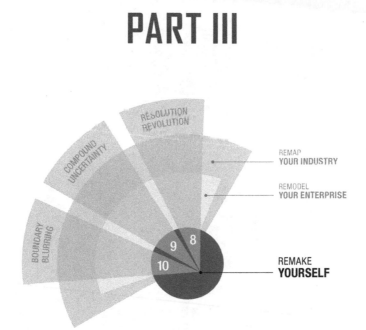

REMAP
YOUR INDUSTRY

REMODEL
YOUR ENTERPRISE

REMAKE
YOURSELF

RESOLUTION REVOLUTION

COMPOUND UNCERTAINTY

BOUNDARY BLURRING

8

Be an Adventurer and an Ambassador

As digital goes to the core of the enterprise—into the very products and services it offers—the resolution revolution's deeply disruptive power challenges persistent norms and deeply rooted beliefs. Leading the team in this context requires an inspiring vision of what's possible, a deep conviction that change is necessary, and an adventurer's zeal for the quest. But to bring everyone along on the digital journey, leaders must couple this adventurer's spirit with an ambassador's art of persuasion and loyalty to the enterprise's ultimate purpose.

A select group of adventurous sailors has circumnavigated the globe. Even fewer have sailed around the world single-handedly. Pete Goss has done both.[1] An adventurer to the core, Goss has visited the North Pole four times, kayaked around Tasmania, and led a crew of novice sailors in what has been called the world's toughest yacht race, the British Steel Challenge, which sends boats the "wrong way around the world" against all the prevailing winds and currents. He may be best known and earned his MBE for rescuing his fellow competitor, Raphael Dinelli, from hurricane-force winds in the Southern Ocean during the 1996–97 Vendée Globe, giving up his position in the race. Goss's story demonstrates an adventurer's zeal to set an inspiring vision as well as the courage to assume a degree of risk on his quest to obtain it.

When he was twenty-four and serving in the British Royal Marines, Goss received a call from his boss. Would he like to compete in a major cross-ocean race? Absolutely, he replied. With only modest sailing experience, Goss saw this as his chance at a big one, the Carlsberg Two-Handed Transatlantic Race from Plymouth, England, to Newport, Rhode Island, in the United States. The subsequent hasty preparation concentrated on refitting a handed-down boat, the *Sarie Marais*, which wasn't quite built for the task. Goss and his fellow sailor worked hard to prepare, logged training miles, and quickly got to know the boat and each other. When it was nearly time to leave, they realized in the hurried planning they had neglected one area of training: they hadn't studied their books on astronavigation properly! How would they find their way across the Atlantic?

Does this feel at all like your situation in response to digital disruption? Your circumstances may have several themes in common: Goss also knew the need, had a desire to move forward, but lacked all knowledge of how to get there.

On the evening before the race began, this pair of novice transatlantic sailors went down to the pub to wrestle with their navigational challenge. Quitting was not an option. In the worst case, they figured they were bound to hit America if they followed the sunsets. Once they were close, they could ask a fisherman whether to turn left or right. Out on the ocean, however, they discovered a better compass. They followed the vapor trails of aircraft flying from London to New York, at least until dense clouds scuttled that plan. Improvising again, they relied on the *Concorde*. If its sonic boom was from the north, they tacked up. If it boomed to the south, they tacked down.

Their improvised navigation system worked. The *Sarie Marais* arrived at the finish and was second in her class. And the race inspired Goss to make a commitment. "During that voyage I decided to compete in a single-handed, 'round the world race," he said. He went on to conquer this further quest. Goss learned how to push on and adapt despite uncertainty, and to remain focused on the goal.

Remake Yourself to Successfully "Challenge the Norm"

As a guest inspirational speaker at a Gartner CIO Academy at Oxford University, Pete Goss shared his perspective that true leadership means "challenging the norm." This stands in stark contrast to management, which he described as making today's model more efficient. For Goss, leadership and risk go hand in hand. While stressing that prudent planning and risk mitigation should always be practiced (learn the navigational techniques ahead of time!), he noted that there are certain situations that require a leader to improvise. "Sometimes you just have to follow your conviction, even in the face of uncertainty and not knowing the exact path,"[2] Goss said. In other words, start before you are fully ready and follow the vapor trails.

Like other navigators, digital leaders must often start before they have all the answers. When it comes to the disruptive territory of exploiting the digital possible, it's often not feasible or prudent to gather all the proof points, the robust evidence for ROI, ahead of time. Speed matters. Yet inherent uncertainty renders "perfect prediction" a fool's game.

Pioneers at the frontier of the resolution revolution must work to design and deliver new products and services in uncharted seas. Leaders in this space must plot a new path. They must therefore be driven in part by a sense of adventure, a desire for an exciting or unusual undertaking with an uncertain outcome. And to bring others along, they must couple an adventurer's spirit with the loyalty and persuasion of an ambassador.

In researching digital leadership and drawing on more than thirty-five interviews with C-level business technology executives, we found that two key leadership personas became clear: adventurer and ambassador. These personas distill common patterns of remaking yourself as a digital leader:

- Muster an adventurer's courage to exploit digital in the face of uncertainty.
- Start outside with relentless customer centricity to identify your digital quest.

- Reset your risk-reward trade-off to reflect new market conditions.
- Display an ambassador's loyalty and powers of persuasion to bring others along.

Muster an Adventurer's Courage

Ford is on another voyage into uncharted waters—to remaster mobility. Ford CEO Mark Fields told us, "As leaders of the organization, we recognize that it starts with us. We have to role model the style and behaviors critical to creating a fast-paced, innovative culture. We need to give the organization permission to think and to act like a start-up company, and ultimately, to disrupt our own business model, before someone else tries to do it for us."[3] Fields said he knows exactly what is at stake for the incumbents in his sector as digital disruption takes hold. Appointed CEO in 2014 at the age of fifty-three, he is the leader who will drive this 112-year-old company through this exciting stage in its journey.

Digital changes, such as the advent of connected cars and autonomous vehicles, require Fields and his team to rethink Ford's basic business model. "We are viewing ourselves as both an auto and a mobility company," noted Fields, who went on to explain what he means by mobility. "At Ford, mobility is about far more than motion or moving from Point A to Point B. It is really about human progress. It involves moving food to the stores you shop in, ambulances arriving at the scene of an accident in time to save a life, or making it to your daughter's recital on time."[4] This will be a difficult and sometimes perilous journey into uncharted waters. No matter how charismatic or good Fields is, he cannot do it alone. He must lead others, and they must operate as a team.

Fields is passionate about the need to drive innovation across the entire team and into every part of the business. "To do this we need to encourage our teams not to take anything for granted as we seek out compelling new opportunities. We must challenge custom and question tradition. We need to engage early, to test, learn, and iterate—and not shy away from uncertainty. We need to give our teams the freedom to move fast and take appropriate risks."[5]

Ford CIO Marcy Klevorn said that as part of her job she needs to have a keen sense of adventure in order to help the company push into new territory: "I firmly believe that anything is possible with the vision and determination to achieve." While she relies on ambassadorial skills foremost, she said, "I'm also a bit of an 'adventurer' in that I thrive on taking smart risks that can drive our business forward. If you don't try, you will never learn, right? I have been known to come up with a 'wild' idea or two, and in these cases I look for those around me to support and evolve the idea, as well as those who will tell me when it's a bit too 'wild'!"[6] Wild is not a word you might expect to hear from a leader of such a massive corporation. It challenges traditional ideas that executives in an engineering-oriented enterprise exercise quiet, commanding control.

When GE decided to make a bold move into the Industrial Internet, CEO Jeffrey Immelt and CTO Mark Little acted with the courage of adventurers to radically change the direction and structure for the company. As Bill Ruh, vice president of GE Software, shared, "They [Immelt and Little] looked and realized that it was not something that you could wait on, and if you look at other industries, by the time it was obvious, it was too late, right? In the music industry, by the time it was obvious, it was too late. In the book business, the same was true."[7]

To institutionalize this type of relevant digital leadership across GE, in early 2015 Immelt oversaw the rollout of a set of behavioral principles called "GE Beliefs." A sample belief is the explicit recognition for the need to "Deliver results in an uncertain world," further described by three key behavioral anchors:

- We act with urgency, and play to win.
- We have the courage to make bets others won't.
- We use expertise and judgment to manage risk while always acting with integrity.[8]

Note the adventurer's traits contained in this belief: deliver on the quest (results matter) while explicitly recognizing the need to tackle uncertainty head on and mustering courage beyond that of others, all while balancing against the inherent risk. This sense of creating courage and encouraging risk taking is key to remaining competitive in the digital era. As Mark Fields at Ford told us, "In the past, we have been somewhat risk averse—in our partnerships, our processes, our willingness to experiment. This is changing rapidly as we embrace a culture of innovation at Ford. Creating an environment that celebrates successes—as well as our failures—will be key to future success."[9]

To go digital to the core, leaders accept that the necessary digital change will often be at odds with conventional wisdom and long-held beliefs. Consider the initial meetings during which Arvind Gupta of India's BJP proposed a 3D hologram to be used at critical election rallies. The BJP realized that avoiding another election loss meant adventuring into new digital territory. Or think of Eric Babolat's mission to change the game of tennis, all the way to the thirty-first rule. Without an adventurer's thirst to discover new possibilities despite inherent uncertainty, leaders will likely conclude that leaving their enterprise's comfort zone is not worth the risk.

Stand back and reflect briefly about being an adventurer like Pete Goss, or being one of the digital business leaders at Ford, facing the future of autonomous cars. Question yourself. How does it make you *feel?* If the feeling is a clear thrill of excitement pulsing through your veins, then you naturally possess the adventurer's zeal. Congratulations! Harness that energy in your digital leadership journey to inspire others, but temper what could be interpreted as overexuberance by emphasizing the ambassadorial persona described later.

Start Outside to Find Your Digital Quest

Consider for a moment a common trait of some of the most successful and disruptive digital-era enterprises that, by the way, represent an immense amount of wealth creation as measured by their market capitalization. Steve Jobs at Apple sought to simplify the user interface and experience. Jeff Bezos at Amazon set out to reinvent the retail shopping experience. Google's Larry Page made it possible to search the world's information. These and other great leaders possessed a vision for a new way of doing something, a vision that challenged the norm, and that others often could not see. They used as their compass an astute outside–in orientation to cast a vision that is deeply customer centric. In essence, they inspired a quest to deliver on the "art of the digital possible."

Mike Giresi, CIO of fashion retailer Tory Burch, acknowledged that people move faster than companies in terms of embracing new technology and changing behavior. That's where an adventurer's outside–in mentality can leverage customer trends to build new products. "I have a team of people who do nothing but work on innovation, and they're incredibly disruptive, so disruptive that culturally sometimes it creates some friction within the organization," he said.[10] Giresi thinks that friction is a good sign, and we agree. Without some friction you won't make any serious progress—digital adventurers are agitators.

Adventurers must be willing to reinvent products and norms to meet customer needs or to exceed their expectations. Think of Volvo Cars's CIO Klas Bendrik, whose customer-centric mind-set helped the company imagine Roam Delivery. "We engaged with real people, real customers in real-life situations," he said. "We engaged with an e-business delivery partner. In this case, groceries, because we knew it would become a weekly delivery pattern." He added, "We also then engaged with a transportation company. They were highly engaged in how these deliveries were actually being made. We actually got this live test and real results, both from a customer's perspective and the supply chain perspective, as well as the e-business perspective."[11] Teams can imagine customer-centric scenarios, but it takes an adventurous leader to move them toward reality.

These fundamental concepts apply equally to the government and public sector. The U.K. Government Digital Strategy is both citizen centric—"We plan and design our services around what users need to get done, not around the ways government want them to do it," said GDS's Mike Bracken[12]—and targets more affordable government that leverages newly feasible digital delivery capabilities. According to the strategy forwarded by member of Parliament Francis Maude, "By going digital by default, the government could save between £1.7 and £1.8 billion each year."[13] Bracken described it as a "strategy from without, not from within,"[14] driven from a starting point of fast-changing citizen needs and external trends, not the inner workings of government.

As digital goes to the core of an enterprise's competitive differentiation, the complexity of the opportunity to remaster products and services can be daunting. Leaders must set a clear direction to focus the energy and exploit digital. As noted in the 2015 Gartner CIO Agenda Report, digital is moving to center stage and increasingly determining winners and losers in every industry and government sector. We asked, in this survey of 2,810 CIOs, if and how this impacts needed leadership skills. A full 75 percent of CIO respondents felt they needed to change their leadership style in the next three years to be successful. And the aspect they felt needed to be dialed up most was a *visionary style*, chosen by 47 percent of respondents.

Viewed through the adventurer's lens, what is the conquest that is worth pursuing? From your perspective as a digital leader, what is the differentiating vision? What is worth expending your personal political capital, reputation, and possibly job to pursue? Each of the digital leaders referenced in this section believed deeply in a particular customer-driven vision and value proposition. This type of vision is essential to success as a digital leader.

Reset Your Risk Orientation

To be a true digital leader, one who makes a real difference at the core of your enterprise, you will need to be brave. There is no skirting that fact. Pete Goss describes leadership as "challenging the norm." Inherent in this definition is uncertainty—movement and action involve risk.

Earlier in this chapter, Mike Giresi, CIO at Tory Burch, explained the need for disruptive innovation, and with that comes risk. The premium fashion brand and retailer wanted to allow each sales associate to carry "clienteling" capabilities on an iPad, yet the application didn't exist. Tory Burch signed a vendor that presented an application that appeared to match the retailer's needs, but it soon became clear that it wasn't quite the right fit for Tory Burch. "We had a decision to make,"

Giresi shared. "We could either scrap the project and deal with the political fallout (which would have happened in my previous lives), or we could press on. We pressed on because the person who was leading the direct-to-consumer group believed the only way to really differentiate against other retailers in our segment was to have a way to allow people who engage with the brand to truly understand not only what they've been doing online or offline but to also allow the sales associates to do that."[15]

The company spent more than $2 million on a program that did not have a clear ROI, but it assumed the risk because, according to Giresi, "We were so passionate and we believed in it and we felt that there were enough associated data points that would prove we were correct." After going live with the program, Tory Burch saw a massive uplift in conversion income for individuals who participate within this application versus those who did not.

"I think it's a testament to the belief that, if there's a better way to do something and it doesn't necessarily exist, then you're going to have to be willing to say, 'I'm going to try this. I don't know if it's going to work but I really believe it could be impactful.' You've got to get behind it," Giresi said.

Risk itself dramatically changes in the digital era as every industry is being remastered. In the 2014 Gartner CIO Survey, 89 percent of respondents felt that the digital world is creating new types and levels of risk for their business, while 69 percent felt that risk management practices are not keeping up with these higher levels of risk, creating greater exposure for their business/entity. Of course, cybersecurity, information privacy, and business continuity concerns are rightly top of mind for every executive today. However, myriad other risk vectors can be more subtle but no less profound or threatening. Missing one of the major tipping points described in chapter 4 can result in a huge customer flight, lost revenue and margin, or an irrelevant business model.

Allied Irish Banks CEO David Duffy reflected for us on what he sees as disruptive changes that will impact the banking sector over the next ten years. He described his organization's need to recognize that it will become a highly technology-driven utility for the business of payment and cash management, and if that's the great portion of the volume in retail, "What's different about that versus how Google operates?" Duffy went on to say:

> Therefore, the premise for success will be around the most advanced possible understanding of your customer using data analytics, just like Google, and understanding how to translate that to cross-sell in a world of mass commoditization. Additionally, banks must protect margins and provide the products and the best customer experience and the best optimization of product on an equivalent cost with equivalent access 24-7, with equivalent easy-to-use technology.
>
> As a CEO, if you want to be transformative in your disposition and develop a strategy in that, you're going to have to take a lot of risk, personally, to drive that agenda. The second thing is, you have to find executives who get the ideas and are of a similar risk-taking nature in terms of their willingness to challenge everything that the waves of tradition try to drown them with and to see beyond that, see beyond the now and beyond the next best, and into the what we need to be if we're going to survive. You've got to have leaders with an intuitive understanding of emerging technologies. They've got to be tech savvy and they've got to be risk oriented and they've got to have vision and passion around the future because this is a huge translation exercise for the institution.[16]

Similarly, in a period rife with digital disruption, failing to tackle a remapping of your core products and services to exploit the art of the digital possible, despite the unknowns and risks, incurs a consummate risk—that of inaction. Digital leaders must ensure visibility of the transformational tipping points most relevant to their industry, then mobilize others to take action. The risk of inaction is also personal. If you don't act, someone else will, and you run the risk of being marginalized from this opportunity space, possibly all the way to losing your job to a leader who brings the "digital chops," risk tolerance, and bias for action.

Digital leaders must force their companies to face reality and take risks. That means understanding how to deal with the risk of project failure, not denying it can happen. Mike Bracken and Russell Davies at the U.K. GDS are passionate about this issue. They say others in government have often said the GDS will fail. Davies said, "Yeah, there will be failure, but there's resilience built into the model. We don't bake in failure as an institutional construct. The moment it takes you two years to write a requirements document, *that's* when you will fail." Bracken added, "We came into existence because of a continued failure of large-scale IT projects. Yes, we'll fail. But we'll fail small and fail quickly; we'll learn from it. At least we have some sort of path out of it—we have some reactive capacity."[17]

Remastering your risk mind-set and methods to reflect new market conditions is imperative. The closer digital moves to the core, the more the stakes and emotions rise. The more digital "challenges the norm," the more leaders need to muster an adventurer's zeal. However, an adventurer without a sense of diplomacy, without links to the enterprise's mission and culture, will likely be viewed as a loose cannon, a weird outlier, or even a pirate! As such, she will be vulnerable to the constant swells and waves of resistance. This resistance often draws from a tide of powerful sentiments: "This is the way we have always done things here," "This is what is driving today's P&L," or plain old "This is what we know."

Bring an Ambassador's Diplomacy to Your Quest

The very best ambassadors exercise diplomacy as an artful balance of social interaction, relationships, communication, persuasion, and understanding of power. As we have stated, digital leaders must have a compelling vision and deep conviction about their particular form of the digital possible, one that is unique to their enterprise's mission and competitive context. But this alone is not enough. It counts for nothing if the leader is not able to impact change or to employ an ambassador's skills and bring others along.

Dr. Hee Hwang, chief information officer and chief medical officer at Seoul National University Bundang Hospital, described his role in translating patient and staff needs to the engineers who can bring innovative technology-enabled processes and treatments to life. "The developers and the engineers are experts in the development of some coding systems, but understanding the end user's requirements is really complicated and very difficult to understand," he said. "My primary role is to act as negotiator or ambassador between engineers and the hospital person, from those at CFO level to the technicians and pharmacists and some staff physicians."[18]

Ford CIO Marcy Klevorn echoed the need to bridge the IT organization with other parts of the business. "I view my main role as linking business and IT strategy, thus the role of ambassador is most relevant for me as the CIO at Ford Motor Company. It provides me the opportunity to create the right environment that is motivating and encouraging."[19]

At GE, Bill Ruh plays an ambassador's role both inside and outside the four walls of GE. Inside the organization, he evangelizes, educates, and models the needed digital mind-sets and behaviors. In doing so, he inspires and galvanizes various business units, teams, and individuals, demonstrating how to think, act, and deliver digitally remastered products and services to the marketplace.

The need for an ambassador is just as great externally. At GE, the role includes helping the GE business units and customers realize the benefits of the Industrial Internet strategy. Ruh has, for the last four years, led a "Minds and Machines" conference designed to share GE's vision and engage the ecosystem of customers and partners around new go-to-market capabilities such as the Predix analytics platform.

While representing a fringe asset of your business strategy may be important, when digital moves to the core of your strategy, championing and instilling confidence externally becomes mission critical. And digital-savvy top leaders are particularly well placed to play an external ambassadorial role, selling the vision, championing the direction, and instilling confidence. When digital moved to the core at Volvo with the connected car, CIO Klas Bendrik, like Ruh at GE, stepped up to represent the brand and help "sell" remastered products such as the XC90 car and associated services externally. Whether under the bright lights of the media launch at a car show or in videos on the digital marketing channel, Bendrik plays an ambassadorial role as Volvo's digital future unfolds.

Underpinning the ability of digital leaders to play such ambassadorial roles and instill confidence in their cause is the perception of their personal brand. And that is in great part derived from what they do, particularly the extent to which they embrace digital technology in both their professional and personal lives.

Role Model "The Art of the Digital Possible"

Allied Irish Banks (AIB) CEO David Duffy described a very real circumstance related to mind-sets and competing for technology talent given the digital marketplace shifts: "What I have to do is be seen almost as an obsessive technologist, and there is a joke about it in the bank now because the new iPhone comes out and guess what? I have it two weeks before it's generally available in Ireland." If you seek to be a world-class digital leader in a traditional enterprise, think of yourself as an envoy representing this new field. As such, find ways to be personally immersed and committed, right at the digital frontier.

At a fundamental level, technology should permeate the way you live your personal life. Whether that is experiencing personal mobility via Uber, Lyft, or similar services rather than a traditional taxi, booking accommodations via Airbnb rather than at traditional hotels, or getting first-look news via Twitter or Reddit rather than newspapers, firsthand "immersive experiences" are vital, both to understand today's state of the art and its pitfalls, but also as a catalyst for your own creative thinking and ideas. This firsthand, experience-based foundation will also be an important determinant of how you are perceived by others.

Over and over, we heard in our research interviews with visionary digital leaders in traditional organizations about their almost obsessive desire to regularly obtain outside–in immersive digital insights and experiences. For example, Ford's CEO Mark Fields, along with the CTO and CIO, visits Silicon Valley on a regular basis to meet with leaders of interest.

Tory Burch, based in New York, values its strategic relationship with Google, which gives it a way to stay close to the latest digital thinking. Executives at the lifestyle brand also visit the West Coast regularly.[20] Ford, McDonald's, Zappos and many other organizations have opened a presence in Silicon Valley (or equivalents globally) to "stay close to the flow of ideas," as Bill Ruh at GE described it.

As we saw in chapter 4, Steve Perry at Visa spends a considerable amount of his time outside the office meeting with start-ups, which helps him explore and understand the digital world. "I can't jive unless somebody is showing me how to jive," he said.[21]

Immersing yourself is one part of being a digital leader, but it is not enough to influence how others perceive you if it is not visible. Of course, the way you communicate matters a great deal. As a leader in a fast-changing environment, every word, all team meeting presentations, and the like will be scrutinized and assessed. However, what you are doing (what you model), rather than just what you are saying, is a more effective form of communicating who you are and what you believe as a digital leader.

Let's return to Marcy Klevorn, CIO at Ford, who is very mindful of her personal brand and consciously role models digital leadership behaviors. She recognizes that "working as a team and ensuring that everyone has all the information they need to do their job is the best way to get results that are effective and long lasting." These characteristics are particularly relevant and valuable in a digital environment. Klevorn described her rationale and approach this way: "I appreciate the change we are all experiencing, as information has become limitless and its immediate availability can create distractions."

One specific area Klevorn changed in 2015 was the way she connects with her global organization. Her new approach is to leverage virtual meetings via the latest video and conferencing tools. Additionally, Klevorn began a series of personal video messages that she records on her iPhone and sends to her entire global team. She strives to balance communicating regularly with respecting her team's time, given the demanding environment. Klevorn noted, "I keep these messages to one minute in length. In fact, they are titled, 'If you have a minute ...' The intent is to foster a sense of 'small' company inside an organization of more than eleven thousand employees. Putting myself out there is also an effort to lead by example—I encourage my team to take risks and not be afraid to fail."

While sitting in her office meeting with one of this book's authors, Klevorn revealed something very poignant and telling. She pulled out of her briefcase a mini flex iPhone tripod to demonstrate the point, and shared how, at the completion of recording a one-minute video, she leaned toward the camera to hit "stop," in true video selfie fashion. Her temptation was then to edit out those last few awkward seconds, but she didn't, favoring the authenticity of a more personal "video selfie" feel over something more produced, modeling the change clearly. In fact, Klevorn has kept that personal touch in each of the weekly videos since.

At the most simple level, leaders are conscious of the topics and messaging with which they open a meeting. Klas Bendrik, CIO at Volvo Cars, explained how he deliberately uses 50 percent of the available time at meetings attended by his CXO peers on both education and strategizing around digital trends that will impact Volvo's business. At another level, David Smoley, CIO of AstraZeneca, makes it mandatory for his direct reports to regularly blog, tweet, personally embrace, and experiment with other digital capabilities in order to become savvier digital leaders. UBS CIO Oliver Bussmann is well known for his blogging style and his willingness to articulate his vision in social media.

In short, live, breathe, and role model the digital change you want to see.

Digital Leaders Bring Others Along

Powerful digital leadership is not for the faint of heart. In many cases, your peers will be blind to the market forces that threaten your space and the digital opportunity available. Alternatively, they may be impeded by mind-set and management behaviors poorly suited to the demands of highly disruptive digital change. As digital moves to the core and the resolution revolution drives great change across primary products and services, this opportunity space demands a particular flavor of leadership.

Fortunately, most successful leaders have at their core many of the necessary leadership traits. With the right orientation and appreciation of the needed change, you can remaster your leadership mix to amplify your digital vision and define a quest that inspires others to join you, despite the uncertainty. Remix your risk–reward trade-off and use an ambassador's persuasion to move forward with courage and conviction.

Actionable Takeaways

Find your compelling digital quest. Start outside, with customer centricity as your compass. Define a vision that inspires others to harness the resolution revolution and remaster your products and services.

Muster courage from your inner adventurer. Strengthen your conviction from the fact that the prevailing digital trends necessitate "challenging the norm." Exhibit courage in the face of uncertainty and deep-seated skeptics.

Remix your risk–reward trade-off. Balance the risk of inaction with the risk of failure in the context of outside–in market forces. Be prepared to start before you have all the answers.

Utilize an ambassador's art of persuasion. Being right counts for nothing if you cannot influence and lead the needed change. Bring others along, at all times staying loyal to your enterprise's ultimate purpose.

Remake yourself to be the digital change you want to see. Live, eat, and breathe digital all the way with immersive learning and idea generation. Demonstrate conviction and passion while understanding others' blind spots.

9

Be a Clarifier and an Educator

Leading in this digital era will be an uncertain endeavor, as techno-logical, social, and regulatory tipping points intertwine and compound upon each other. As the level of industry disruption increases, it becomes ever more critical that digital leaders be clarifiers of what matters most, including both the threats and opportunity spaces at the confluence of the specific tipping points most critical to their enterprise. In addition to being clarifiers, effective digital leaders must play a key role as educators to amplify digital savvy in the C-suite and board and to upgrade the digital DNA of the wider enterprise. The digital leader's task is not only to help others grasp the digitally enabled differentiation capabilities, but also to encourage the new mind-sets and skills needed to lead in this persistently uncertain, high-velocity, and innovation-driven era.

Krischa Winright sat in her office and thought about the best way to clarify her message. As chief information officer at Priority Health and vice president of information technology at Spectrum Health, an integrated health system in Michigan, Winright knew that her presentation to the board would determine the company's next step in digital innovation. What was the best way to convince both Priority Health and its parent company, Spectrum Health, to fund her bold initiative?

Winright reviewed the presentation materials she had prepared to convince the executives to move from a lagging reporting structure to predictive analytics. Could dozens of executives be induced to support such a significant investment, given their diverse accountabilities and organizational strategies? How could she help them understand the opportunity at stake?

Winright remembered the last board update and how she had been struck by the years of clinical and administrative experience the board members represented. She couldn't oversimplify or overcomplicate her proposal. It had to be the perfect blend of information and inspiration. Then she thought of something. Winright remembered the large stack of reports that represented the company's current analytics capability. She decided to take an approach completely different from the one she'd been planning.

The next day, when Winright addressed the executive team, she began her presentation by unfolding a large paper road map. She asked board members to recall the days of using printed travel maps to find their way to a new destination. She pointed out the limitations of these earlier techniques and got a few laughs. First, she noted, it was easiest if someone was reading the map for you, so a passenger came in handy. (Winright wanted the executives to see how reliant they were on others—like report writers—to run their business.) She also joked about the risks of navigating to locations that fell on the creases in any of the map's folds. And, she reminded them, if anything went wrong on the route, you ended up on the side of the road or at a gas station asking for more help.

Then Winright took the board on a journey through time from paper maps to digital navigation. Drivers were able look up a map online and get directions. They could print the directions. Mapping software indicated the quickest route and provided step-by-step instructions along the way. "But," she continued, "I will never forget the day my GPS talked to me. I was headed down the interstate on a very long trip, and out of the blue a voice said, 'In ten miles there will be a twenty-minute delay. Would you like to take an alternate route?' In amazement, I spoke back aloud to the GPS, 'Now *that* was helpful!'"

Winright paused and reached under the table to retrieve the six-inch-thick paper management report. It contained each potential care opportunity for the entire patient population. Quietly, with great purpose and intention, she set the report on the boardroom table and simply reminded the group of its contents. The silence around the table was stunning, she recalled. Each executive understood the correlation, and knew that the company was running its business on the equivalent of an old road map. And the board understood the human impact if they did nothing to change that model. They approved Winwright's requested analytics investment before she left the room.[1]

Remake Yourself As an Amplifier of Digital Savvy

As a digital leader, one who is fully immersed and always probing digital trends and their impact on your enterprise, you will often be several steps ahead of your peers in your thinking. This mismatch can form a dangerous chasm, made more treacherous by the compound uncertainty of the technological, social, and regulatory tipping points discussed in chapter 3. The best digital leaders do not bemoan the dynamic of "why others don't get it" but rather tackle it head-on, embracing a collaborative role that is part clarifier and part educator.

A key place to start is with the sometimes bewildering effects of the compound uncertainty associated with digital disruption. The goal of the digital leader is to remake or flip the mind-set from one that views uncertainty as a paralyzing force to one that sees uncertainty as source of opportunity. Macroeconomics tells us that stable markets, moving on linear trajectories and characterized by relative certainty, translate to fierce competition and low margins. But what about markets buffeted by compounded uncertainty, by waves of tipping points so disruptive they can change the competitive structure across industries? If viewed through the lens of a venture capitalist or Silicon Valley entrepreneur, these disruptions can represent the opportunity of a lifetime. If viewed through the lens of a more traditional corporate leader, they represent a mesmerizing conundrum: they are too important to ignore but are simultaneously perplexing due to the inherent uncertainty found at every turn!

Leaders who feel overwhelmed by the myriad questions and choices that digital presents are not alone. While uncertainty is a future reality, the traditional leadership belief systems, mind-sets, and behaviors that many have honed during times of more stable markets can be an even bigger impediment to success. Instead, leaders need to remake thought patterns and practices that pigeonhole uncertainty as bad and hone personal leadership to fully embrace uncertainty as opportunity. Effective digital leaders remake their leadership to not only capitalize on the immense opportunity when tipping points coalesce, but to clarify the advantages and educate others on how to move forward.

Part of a leader's mandate in today's climate is to clarify how to think about digital disruption, its most important aspects to her specific enterprise's context, and the big bets that need to be made. Digital leaders need to educate other leaders and the organization about how to respond to the opportunity space in ways that are "fit for digital purpose." And they must do this in the face of inherent and compounded uncertainty—indeed, to succeed, they must provide a path forward that embraces uncertainty as a friend. The clarifier–educator role embodies five essential tasks:

1. Clarify digital opportunity and direction to meet desired outcomes.
2. Flip beliefs to lead and win by embracing uncertainty.
3. Use experimentation as a tool to deal with uncertainty.
4. Educate and instill digital savvy into the enterprise DNA.
5. Master immersive "show, don't tell" learning techniques.

Harness the Power of Clarity

When Krischa Winright presented her plans to the board, she had in mind a bigger purpose than gaining approval for a specific initiative. She wanted to open board members' minds to the new possibilities that digital capabilities would enable in their business. And she wanted to do it in a way that was easy to embrace, and that clarified why investing and making progress in this direction was essential, even if the executives wouldn't know all the details yet. She wanted to inspire others to join her on an incredibly important digital health-care journey, and since that day in 2013, Winright has made it a priority to clarify, educate, and collaborate with her executive team and board partners on how to maximize the digital opportunity space. So should you.

To start this effort, you may need to help others break free from the sometimes paralyzing effects of ever-present uncertainty. In an environment that presents a bewildering array of digital possibilities learning how to sort hype from reality really matter. Leaders need to educate others about what is, or what will be, possible—perhaps sooner than they realize. Great digital business leaders help those around, below, and above them—the CEO, board, senior executives, and other team members—grasp the opportunity space that matters. In this chapter, we distill some of the key patterns and observations from our research in order to help you become a clarifier and educator and enable others to grasp the digitally enabled opportunity space before them.

Recently, one of your authors—Graham—facilitated a workshop at one of Gartner's European CIO Leadership Forums. The diverse group of executives represented Finland, France, Germany, Ireland, Spain, and the U.K., across industries ranging from financial services to government to health care, manufacturing, and retail. For this exercise, the CIOs were asked to select from ten future-oriented leadership skills which ones they believed would most impact their success if they could master them going forward.[2]

Would this group's results validate the same skills selected by six similar workshops held in the Americas and Asia? After tallying the votes, the answer was clear: the same pattern had played out again for the top two skills. Number one was clarity, specifically as defined by Bob Johansen, distinguished fellow at the Institute for the Future: "The ability to see through messes and contradictions to a future that others cannot yet see."[3]

The ensuing discussions illuminated why this skill was deemed so critical and consistently ranked number one by CIOs. First, many of the CIOs felt their enterprises were experiencing "deer in the headlights" confusion caused by the daunting array of digitally enabled choices. CIOs were often paralyzed by their enterprises' outdated management mind-sets and systems, which were ill-suited to cope with the uncertainty of today's marketplace. The power of bringing clarity to this situation resonated strongly with them.

The CIOs were buoyed, even liberated, by the way the skill was further defined: leaders who embody this type of clarity are very "clear about what they are making, but very flexible about how it gets made."[4] They gained insight and confidence from the combination of the need to be clear about "what you are making"—in our case, the art of the digital possible, often expressed in terms of the desired business capabilities and outcomes—with the expectation that they won't know every nuance of how the scenarios will play out.

If we return to Krischa Winright's road maps example, we can see that she was clear that progress had to be made regarding particular patient outcome goals via predictive analytics even if she didn't know every detail of how to achieve those goals. Or think of our GE example, in which the company distilled macro trends to identify the immense "Industrial Internet" tipping point, and made the bet to grasp early mover advantage without having the entire playbook complete. Or consider BJP's belief that social marketing techniques and 3D holograms were key to communicating the party's core messages to the masses without initially knowing the exact formula for ultimate success.

We also heard repeatedly that the old approach—in which the launch of a huge strategic endeavor entailed a year spent figuring out program requirements and several more years developing the solution—is doomed from the very start.

Flip Beliefs to Lead and Win

The changes that digital business brings can be so deep that some previous management beliefs must be completely inverted. For example, perhaps your company needs to move from products to services. Or perhaps you need to get close to the consumer when previously your agreed model has been to support and empower resellers. You may need to start investing a lot more money into technology after a decade of deliberately trying to reduce such costs.

A digital business leader tests core beliefs of the enterprise on a regular basis, at times even inverting key underlying historic assumptions.
The purpose is not to lack discipline or to be contrarian, however. The
value of the exercise is in repeatedly checking that the organization is
not resting on false assumptions or defending walls that are paper thin.
In team meetings, regularly, gently, but persistently ask "Why?" Why
can't we do more direct selling? Why can't we be a technology company? Why can't we ask customers to pay for services? What are the
underlying reasons for those "rules"? Often the practices had a rational
basis years earlier but have been unquestioned since. The world has
changed, and so must the logic of your firm.

This brings us to a second remarkably consistent series of aha
moments from Graham's workshops around the globe; these concerned the competency of experimentation (or "rapid prototyping," in
Johansen's ten skills)[5] in a business model and business capability context. Experimentation was ranked second on the list of future-oriented
skills in nearly every workshop. During the workshop breakout, CIOs
constantly referred to clarity in combination with experimentation. As
one member at a rapid prototyping breakout session said, "We assumed
we had clarity of purpose and then used rapid prototyping to make it
happen, constantly experimenting, failing fast, and allowing the customer or market to help us find the winning model." A member of the
clarity breakout session said, "We need to define clarity first, but at a
more macro 'outcome-based' level; then we will employ rapid prototyping to help us fine-tune the implementation over time." Across the
workshops, attendees confirmed the ways in which clarity and experimentation mutually reinforce each other.

Pure-play digital companies, particularly as they mature and scale,
have this clarity of purpose (unique customer value proposition) coupled with rapid prototyping. But traditional leaders who have grown
up and anchored their success on more traditional "figure it all out first"
beliefs can find such a fundamental mind-set change difficult. Ten or
fifteen years ago, the business and technology tools and methods for
making progress through prototyping and iteration were uncommon.
Today, they are much easier to harness.

Use Experimentation As Clarity's Friend

Clarity, complemented by experimentation, applies at many levels. Consider an example from online travel-booking business Orbitz. The user experience on the Orbitz website, particularly in key business outcome metrics such as "visitor to buyer conversion rate," is absolutely fundamental to its success. With that clarity, CTO Roger Liew and the Orbitz team relentlessly test new website design ideas leveraging A/B testing. This entails running a percentage of the website traffic through a "challenger" design and simply letting the website visitors determine the champion. This method contrasts with the traditional "waterfall" approach, in which the most senior people make final decisions, define requirements, hold focus groups, develop, implement, and then cross their fingers, legs, and everything else while they hope to drive the desired improvement. Of course, the digital world not only makes A/B experimentation possible, it makes such testing relatively easy.

The power of this leadership mind-set flip was highlighted when Orbitz added some spice and gamified its daily A/B testing. Each test was described on the company's intranet, and users could vote on which they believed would be more successful, A or B. This created great energy and focused the entire organization on what matters most: website performance, key business outcomes, and customers. Employees checked back to see if their choice had won and if they'd qualified for prizes and recognition in the league table as part of their daily routine. But the really illuminating moment came when the analytics team dug into the profiles of those employees who were most successful at predicting the winning designs. There was absolutely no correlation between those who were best at predicting winners and those who were at the top of the organizational hierarchy. This was a simultaneously liberating and challenging revelation to the senior leadership.

As the experimentation competency ramped up at Orbitz, the A/B testing velocity grew to hundreds a year and challenged Liew to make the process an order of magnitude faster to get even faster results. The team evolved the platform with more automation and used different types of statistics to essentially let the tests run by themselves. "It's a constant evolution," Liew said. "The pace of this space means that what we were doing just two years ago feels like a very long time ago."[6]

Raghu Krishnamoorthy, chief learning officer and head of executive development at GE, provided us with another great example of remaking leadership mind-sets and capabilities to match the speed and uncertainty of today's digital marketplace. He used the goal of a new ultrasound machine to contrast previous and current approaches:

> In the past, what we would've said is, "Here is $100 million. Go and prepare the world's best ultrasound machine, and three years later, we will launch it." That would've been a pretty typical play. Now we're saying, "No. We're going to give you $10 million. Develop a prototype. Go and ask the customers whether they like what they see. If they like it, continue to the next stage. If not, change your strategy." You don't lose $100 million before you learn it's not going to be successful in the marketplace. You use the $10 million to experiment and learn what works and what doesn't work for the customer.
>
> Secondly, you need to keep in mind, our customers now ask for increased customization. What is relevant in China may not be relevant in Calgary or in Russia or in the United States. How will you then adjust and accommodate for the nuances of each of these marketplaces?[7]

Krishnamoorthy went on to describe how GE is tackling its journey to upgrade digital savvy on many fronts, including bringing in key executives from outside who are now "teaching us a lot about how we will be able to use Internet and digital thinking as a multiplier going forward and what it looks like for us."[8] Bill Ruh, head of GE Software, is one of those leaders, coming to GE from Cisco and bringing digital savvy from a successful career based mostly in Silicon Valley.

Ruh described some of the thinking he is bringing to GE as he builds out key Predix platform products as part of the company's Industrial Internet strategy:

You have to have an approach that is very different than the traditional big company approach which is...we'll invest, how much return am I going to see, when am I going to see that return. You have to have more of the start-up mentality of a minimally viable product learning from the market and driving it to scale. That's very different than traditional big companies often budget, manage, and deliver on this kind of program.

The second big thing is how you get people to realize that speed and quality and the ability to pivot are more important than planning and getting a fully functional spec and delivering the perfect product to the market. Getting these new processes in place that complement that org shift, the culture shift, are really important, and I always tell people, "Speed wins over full functionality on any given day so you'd rather go faster than try to get everything right."[9]

As these examples illustrate, digital leaders need to be clarifiers, first focusing relentlessly on providing the needed clarity about what they are making and what matters most while being flexible about how it is made. They leverage techniques like experimentation, rapid prototyping, or minimum viable product (MVP) to unleash creativity and talent while letting customers and market forces help determine the winning models. They adapt and learn, then do it again and again.

While this thinking is obvious to digitally savvy leaders, it is counter to the core mind-sets and practices of many leaders who grew up in a more certain, steady, and analog world. Digital leaders should never underestimate nor get frustrated by this dynamic, instead embracing the opportunity to lead by being an educator who helps others grasp the digital opportunity space they cannot yet see.

Educate to Instill a Digitally Savvy Enterprise DNA

Never before have leaders lacking digital savvy run a greater risk of being blindsided by the next technology-enabled tipping point. As we described in chapter 6, Raghu Krishnamoorthy, GE's chief officer, is focused on making sure that the pace of change in organization matches, or in some cases is ahead of, the pace of change outside because otherwise, as he put it, "You will always play catch-up as opposed to lead the change."

GE's solution to build "digital muscle" into the enterprise takes the form of what it calls FastWorks, the company's version of a lean start-up approach that uses rapid prototyping to put an MVP in front of customers. Krishnamoorthy emphasized the need for both a "technical tool kit" and "cultural framework" to effect this type of change within a large organization. "For GE's leaders to pivot their mind-set, you also need to change their frame of thinking. That's what the GE Beliefs help in doing [see chapter 10]. It's a systematic, more holistic approach to the change. It's not one lever or two levers, it's the whole organization with all the tools available for us, technical and cultural, making the strategic shift."[10]

During Gartner's 2014 CIO Agenda development process, our colleague Dave Aron, vice president and Gartner Fellow, uncovered a fascinating pattern in the CIO survey data. Those CIOs who ranked highest on questions that indicate a high-performing IT organization (i.e., most satisfied stakeholders, increasing level of influence, rising budgets) were remarkably correlated to the most positive answers to another of the survey questions, which essentially asked: "How digitally savvy is your CEO?"

Talking to many of these leading CIOs as he pursued more detailed case studies, Aron described the way they thought of their leadership role: "Sure, I have to run a solid IT shop, but even more important is educating and inspiring business peers in the C-suite as to what is possible."

In Gartner's 2015 CIO Agenda survey research, we therefore asked CIOs about the most effective techniques for educating executives and helping increase their digital savvy. Rising to the fore were techniques such as study tours, technology showcases, hackathons that produced contextualized prototypes, and reverse mentoring, all approaches that involve immersive learning in some form.

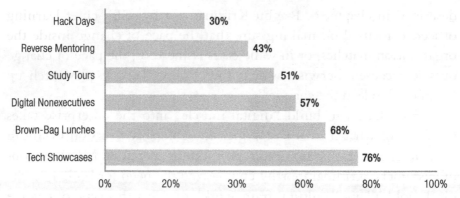

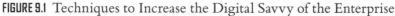

FIGURE 9.1 Techniques to Increase the Digital Savvy of the Enterprise

Show to Educate and Immerse—Don't Tell

Discussions with digital leaders who were successful as educators further emphasized the power of doing and showing, rather than pontificating or telling. Mike Bracken, executive director of digital, U.K. Government Cabinet Office, is passionate about the need to show colleagues how a problem can be tackled or an untapped opportunity space identified. The way that he communicates this belief to those around him exemplifies the principle: "I have a large poster on the wall of my office which says, 'Show the thing,' which is a really shorthand way of saying, 'If you've got a problem, build a prototype of the solution. Come in and show us the prototype, don't write a massive report about the problem and how you might solve the solution.' We just say, 'Show the thing.'"[11] (See figure 9.2.)

This "show don't tell" principle is applicable to a wide variety of situations, to educate and inspire others in the organization about how to:

- Digitally remaster products, services, and customer experience
- Win in an increasingly uncertain world
- Look for the critical tipping points and "art of the digital possible"
- Lead in a new way, leveraging "fit for digital-era purpose" techniques

FIGURE 9.2 Poster in Mike Bracken's office
Source: UK Government Digital Service

Priority Health CIO Krischa Winright, whose story opened this chapter, has only become more passionate about her role as an educator since the day in the boardroom that she showed her road map and her six-inch stack of management reports. As Priority Health pioneers digital leadership across multiple fronts, rolling out patient portals and real-time analytics and competing for new customers in the emergent U.S. health-care exchange markets, Winright is constantly working with her peers to cocreate the winning models and capabilities.

One area that the health-care payer team felt represented a potential market opportunity was "transparency." Consider a patient in need of a hip replacement. Could Priority Health provide an online shopping experience that allowed the patient to understand the fair-market price for that service, together with the quality outcomes of candidate hospitals and providers, in a way that let the patient make the most informed decision? The team sought to simultaneously help Priority Health drive down the cost of health care and improve patient outcomes. There was clarity about the desired outcomes, but uncertainty was everywhere! The organization had vastly different levels of understanding of the opportunity space, the implications to the core business, and the possibilities—would customers be ready for a tipping point and adopt a solution, if it could be provided?

Winright and her team embraced the role of educators. Leveraging their digital experience, they started to cocreate with key visionary leaders, producing renderings of what an Amazon-like shopping experience for a hip replacement might look like. Working back and forth, visualizing and showing ideas, they then expanded to other parts of the business process. They explored what was needed in the "cost estimator" to make estimates accurate for patients based on where they lived, their current health-care coverage, etc. They mocked up screens, which led to working prototypes, multidisciplinary collaboration sessions, and executive reviews.

Once her CEO saw an iteration that he felt was compelling, Winright was asked to make another trip to the boardroom, this time with a prototype (not under the desk but on the screen) that showed how Priority Health could bring a pioneering "health-care transparency digital shopping experience" to the newly implemented health-care marketplace. Once again, the board interaction leaned heavily toward education. "The amazing thing about the experience with 'transparency' was I hardly had to ask for the funding—the opportunity was obvious to all. And rather than having to solicit support, cap in hand, after a prototype session or showcase, people would approach the team and want to be a part of the marketing or customer experience, asking, 'How can we be support the success?'"[12]

Help Others Grasp the Art of the Digital Possible

Arvind Gupta was instrumental in bringing digital to the core of India's Bharatiya Janata Party, and then to its successful 2014 election campaign process. When we asked why other political parties did not

harness similar digital capabilities, Gupta's respons[e]
fact that those other parties did not possess the same d[ ] ult[ ]
did BJP develop this expertise and instill confidence i[ ]

Gupta described a steady journey that started sh[ ]
2009 election loss, and began by first identifying "te_____gy or the
future." Then, in 2010, the party started investing in and evangelizing for the use of those technologies. Workers from the lowest to the
highest levels were trained, creating the platform that Gupta believes
contributed to BJP's victory in 2014. The platform was dependent on
a foundation of social and digital media, on a committed set of volunteers throughout the country, and on data. "The data was critical and
built up over four and a half years," Gupta said.

We asked Gupta what led to the digital traction. "Number one was
the fact that we were able to show tangible outcomes," Gupta recalled.
He described in earlier days being the "lone voice standing." But critical to education and instilling confidence were early wins: "Before
we came to the final match we played a lot of league games, lots of
quarterfinals, semifinals, before we won the final," he said. Whether
experimenting with an Internet TV channel, crowdsourcing a state-
level vision in 2012 (which produced more than 100,000 meaningful
responses), or launching online fund-raising (which it was the first to
do in India), "people saw the outcomes, senior leadership saw the outcomes. I think that also gave us our digital culture and DNA." Gupta
said he believes that slowly it started sinking in with other parties, too,
and they started playing catch-up in 2013, "but they were too late,
we had the three- to four-year advantage of building the foundations
correctly."[13]

Eventually, in May 2014, the BJP assembled an election campaign
twenty-item tool kit that derived from clarity of purpose coupled with
many iterations and innovations, experimentation that identified the
technologies, and methods that would truly "move the needle." Ultimately, according to Gupta, it helped Prime Minister Narendra Modi
win victory and political power.

Gupta at BJP, Bracken at U.K. Government, Winright at Priority Health, and others featured in this chapter all embrace the impor-
tance of educating and helping others first see, then gain clarity, and

...mately realize advantage from digital-enabled capability. Consider how you can remake yourself as a clarifier and an educator to help others in your enterprise grasp the digital opportunities they may not being seeing today.

Actionable Takeaways

Make being a clarifier a key personal leadership focus and competency. Help separate reality from hype and relevant opportunity from the fog of prevailing uncertainty and the noise of deep digital disruption. Drive a focus on desired outcomes to help others find their digital way.

Champion mind-sets and approaches suited to uncertainty and their "fit for digital purpose." Leverage experimentation and other methods to rapidly probe, learn, and adapt. Repeatedly challenge fundamental beliefs that may be dated, then look to flip some of them.

Master and practice immersive learning techniques. Enable personal discovery by others, helping them find the digital opportunities they cannot yet see.

Educate to amplify digital savvy and instill confidence. Combine clarity of focus and real-world learning to upgrade digital until it becomes core enterprise DNA.

10

Be an Attractor and a Cartographer

To compete on the digital-era playing field, leaders need boundary-spanning digital competencies. Powering those competencies requires digitally savvy talent. Digital leaders remake themselves to become attractors of both the best talent and the best ideas. But that alone is not enough. To retain these top people, and to unleash their potential to deliver on digital's promise, leaders must remap existing thinking, spaces, and structures. Digital leaders must remake themselves as cartographers of the new digital-era landscape. They remap internal structures so digital competences can deliver remastered products and services. They remap external competitive marketplace spaces to help their enterprise seize advantage in ways that exploit the new contours of digital business.

Marco Bressan, chairman of BBVA Data & Analytics, regularly welcomed small groups of data scientists and entrepreneurs to the Spanish multinational bank's modern innovation center in Madrid. Bressan had a series of Thursday morning meetings that he relished—each week he invited the winners and interesting entrants from the bank's recent "Innova Challenge."[1] Bressan had designed the innovation challenge as an open competition to attract ideas and talent based on the bank's data, and it drew more than eight hundred developers, who created more than 150 "applications."

At one such meeting, a small collective of entrepreneurs brought together complementary disciplines, all centered on a specific idea inspired during the competition and mined from the bank's data. The idea was to create a service to assist small retailers with the optimal placement of commercial locations. If you were looking to open a shoe shop in Madrid, for example, the service would, based on advanced analytics, assist you in selecting your location and help you understand the type of customers and competitors you should expect. These Thursday meetings were rich with fresh insights that unlocked value from the bank's data with the help of talented people who brought great creativity, passion, and skill.

Bressan recalled another inspiring moment at the innovation center, this time with a group of his BBVA business peers. There was quite a "wow" factor the first time they could see the bank's data creatively overlaid on a map, producing a fascinating visualization of payment patterns across a city and the changes in consumer behavior at night or at various times of day. One insight from the visualization was that a particular restaurant drew people from long distances, past many other seemingly similar restaurants. This turned out to be a very valuable finding and an indicator of "commercial health" for small businesses. That discovery led to the bank incorporating this type of data as an additional viable in its credit-scoring models.

Whether the opportunity is improving the core bank's scoring models or discovering patterns via advanced analytics to enter new businesses, Bressan knows he needs the very best data science and related digital talent to deliver on the possibilities. Attracting top talent had all too often been frustrating, particularly when BBVA was trying to entice talent away from a pure digital enterprise. That's one of the reasons BBVA decided to create its Data & Analytics group as a standalone entity with its own entrepreneurial culture and innovative, data-driven mission.

The data innovation challenge was another creative way to draw in the right profile of analytics talent. Those informal Thursday sessions not only were a source of ideas, they often led to more discussions. The BBVA Data & Analytics entity eventually hired some of the developers, formed a few joint ventures, and found creative ways of working with developers on a contract basis. Bressan said, "We used some of our corporate assets—our own data and its potential—as an attractor for talented data scientists. We functioned more like a start-up than a traditional bank. Notably, we created a culture at BBVA Data & Analytics where someone from Facebook would want to work, a significant achievement in contrast with previous failed experiences attracting top notch data scientists to a traditional bank."

But attracting great talent and ideas is not sufficient to unleash their full potential. Not if existing structures and boundaries are ill suited to the new profiles of opportunity. In this regard, Bressan thinks like a modern cartographer, exploring with his colleagues how to remap the bank's world to leverage new data-enabled innovations in ways that exploit the new contours of digital-era business and ultimately deliver results more rapidly.[2]

Find and Unleash the Full Potential of Talent

The more digital goes to the core of an enterprise, the more the enterprise's vitality depends on digitally savvy talent. In a world where boundaries blur and continuously morph at every level, the winning mind-set of digital leaders in traditional enterprises is not one dominated by command and control, organizational silos, or the boundaries of the enterprise's four walls. Rather, a digital leader with a winning mind-set is part attractor of the best talent and part cartographer, remapping spaces to unleash creativity, ultimately delivering on the digital promise.

As a digital leader, you must be an attractor of the very best talent and the very best ideas that are tightly aligned with your specific digital purpose and sources of marketplace differentiation. You, acting alone, will never be as smart as the "crowd," and certainly you won't be able to execute as quickly. And you need to attract needed talent not only in a one-off hiring transaction or innovation challenge, but in a way that is both sticky and enduring. You need to lead in a way that unleashes the power of ideas and realizes the value of digital while ensuring your people feel fulfilled and inspired to drive sustained results and impact.

This must all occur at the externally mandated clock speed of the marketplace. You must also be a cartographer who can map and remap the evolving digital market space and associated winning enterprise capability space. In essence, the four actions for amassing the right talent in a culture that delivers on the art of the digital possible are:

- Reinvent yourself as a magnet for talent and ideas
- Define and radiate your digital purpose
- Remake a "fit for digital purpose" culture
- Remap internal and external spaces to deliver on the digital promise

Reinvent Yourself as a Magnet for Talent and Ideas

We like to use the analogy of the digital leader as a magnet that emits a strong attracting force. But the best digital leaders don't attract just any people; the trick is to attract people who are already attuned to the leader's and enterprise's core purpose and critical differentiation space, which we think of as the "magnetic true north." Once the right people are in place, it's important to further energize them based on a clear purpose, values, and beliefs. Consider Bressan's adept use of an open data innovation challenge to draw in specific skills and people. Or his creation of an advanced analytics environment as a stand-alone entity with a unique culture designed not only to attract but also to provide a fulfilling space for this talent.

A common theme among digital leaders with the mind-set of attractors is a relentless focus on creating an optimum work environment. The retailer Zappos, already admired for its culture and work environment, does not rest on its laurels. In September 2013, the company moved into a new corporate campus designed to facilitate collaboration at all levels, including a physical design intended to encourage "collisionable moments, where employees bump into one another." But beyond the physical environment, John Peretiatko, senior director of IT, described his thought process regarding talent: "Beyond the stables of salary, benefits, and work space, a lot of what is rewarding for people is to work on something that they're truly passionate about. A lot of my job, a lot of senior tech leadership's job, is helping align people with projects that they're passionate about and letting them self-direct and create their own path. That's how we try to attract talent, and it's been very successful."[3] In April 2015, CEO Tony Hsieh stated in *Zappos Insights Blog* an acceleration towards more self-organization, a move that will further refine the type of talent he seeks to attract.

Geographic hotbeds of technology innovation around the globe are also top of mind, and represent a key component of many digital leaders' attractor strategy. GE, for example, located its software business in San Ramon, California, both to attract the kind of talent that knows how to operate at "Internet speed" and to tap into the ecosystem that exists in the Silicon Valley area.

Similarly, when Ford opened its latest Research and Innovation Center in Palo Alto, California, CEO Mark Fields described it as "designed to bring in new talent and fresh thinking on all of the Ford Smart Mobility plan elements." In combination with offering desirable physical environment, Fields, like Bressan at BBVA, conducts open innovation challenges designed in part to attract specific digital ideas and skills. Ford ran twenty-five global mobility innovation experiments in 2015 to help learn more, collect data, and create affordable and accessible solutions to some of the world's greatest mobility challenges.

For many leaders, a fundamental first step entails a mind-set flip to fully embrace the deeply personal role they must play as an attractor of the "right" talent. To do this, they must articulate and radiate what they seek in a way that draws in the "best fit" people.

Define and Radiate Your Digital Purpose

Beyond a threshold level of income and benefits, top talent works for the buzz, the challenge, or the cause, and not just for the money. Being part of something worthwhile that is bigger than oneself is a powerful driver at the deepest level of our human DNA. Great digital leaders use this innate desire to attract top talent, tapping into this force by being a mission maker or providing a compelling purpose. The good news is that, in an era rife with digital disruption, there is vibrant opportunity to carve out new purposes that matter.

In some pure-play digital enterprises, the company's purpose is the very essence of the entire organization. In other, more traditional enterprises, a new purpose may be a rallying cry for reinvention of the entire enterprise or may act as a catalyst or incubator at the level of the digital team. Whatever the approach, the digital leader who cannot create and communicate a compelling purpose will find it hard to attract the needed talent and support to succeed. Consider the following two examples of leadership founded on a compelling purpose.

Arvind Gupta, innovation evangelist and information and technology head of India's BJP, described the party's vision for a "digital India" that includes a billion connected citizens. The party already leverages crowdsourcing techniques that facilitate participative governance and further "digital democracy."[4] In a June 2014 speech, Prime Minister Narendra Modi pledged to build one hundred smart cities across India, describing the technology enablement in this way: "Cities in the past were built on riverbanks. They are now built along highways. But in the future, they will be built based on availability of optical fiber networks and next-generation infrastructure."[5] Modi offers a fine example of inspiring a digital purpose.

Quicken Loans CIO Linglong He described the company's central purpose as digitizing the loan origination process (Quicken Loans' core business) in the same way Amazon digitized the book business and YouTube digitized the video business. Her personal purpose was around people. "My passion is for people, to help them grow and for team members to help our business grow," Lingong He said.[6]

Digital purpose must be backed up with real substance in order for talent to be attracted to it. It must involve a coherent strategic approach, the necessary investment, and an appealing physical work environment. But discerning talent will look beyond these tangibles to the softer issues. They'll ask, "Is this a digital leader who inspires me to want to work for him? Do this company and leader 'get it' digitally? Is the culture digitally forward, and will it attract others like me and allow us to succeed?" After all, everyone wants to be fulfilled at work and be part of a winning team.

Remake a "Fit for Digital Purpose" Culture

Peter Drucker is credited with saying "Culture eats strategy for breakfast." This statement is a fitting reminder of just how powerfully culture can counter change; entrenched cultural beliefs may be rooted deep in the organizational psyche, and can act like the human immune system, attacking cells at the very core of the body. As digital increasingly moves to the heart and soul of the organization, the opportunity space and need for change are very obvious to most digital leaders. However, it's important for these leaders to remember that many in the broader organization will be at varying points on that "need for change" journey. This fact may lead to immensely powerful cultural resistance, which may be fully capable of eating your fledgling digital strategy for breakfast.

If a traditional and increasingly less relevant culture prevails, however, it may stifle, slow, or even snuff out your digital progress. This halting of progress may create a downside risk of marketplace irrelevance even greater than the inherent uncertainty associated with the digital future. Just consider the number of "Kodak-like" company demises, in which the culture's inability to adapt to new market-force realities or to embrace new competitive behaviors contributed to the company's downfall. As in the early digital *Pac-Man* game (which had the goal of eating while avoiding being eaten), there is a bigger predatory force in the market. Think of this principle as "Digital disruptive market forces will consume enterprises with irrelevant cultures as a snack."

What does a "fit for digital purpose" culture look like?

Let's take a glimpse into a workplace recognized by *Computerworld* as the number one place to work in IT (large company category) in both 2013 and 2014,[7] and rated by *Forbes* as among the top five places to work in 2014. Quicken Loans was the largest online loan originator in the United States and ranked highest in the J.D. Power customer satisfaction survey in its sector for the last five years; this company is rapidly growing in both absolute and market-share dimensions.

When asked about the secret behind this success, CIO Linglong

He didn't miss a beat: "Bottom line is, culture creates everything. Quicken Loans is about culture, culture, culture. If you do not create the culture it will be created for you."[8] In Quicken Loans' case the culture is driven right from the top, from founder Dan Gilbert, who emphasizes the company's ideals with new employees at a two-day orientation that Dan and CEO Bill Emerson personally attend.

The "secret sauce" of Quicken Loans' culture is articulated in a set of nineteen ideals called "ISMs," which describe as much about "who the company is" as "what they do." An example of an ISM is "You'll see it when you believe it," elaborated as: "Do you believe it? Then you can make it happen. It doesn't work the other way round. When you believe in something, you will find a way to get it done. You can and will affect the outcome...if you truly believe.[9]" The nineteen ISMs work together to define a culture designed to attract great talent and unleash ideas and innovation while also driving breakthrough customer service and business results.

It is critical that the culture attracts the right type of people, but it must also personally fulfill those people and inspire them to maximize their contribution. Linglong He describes innovation as part of Quicken Loans' DNA. Indeed, she champions "Bullet Time," a weekly four-hour period every Monday after 1 p.m. During this time, the entire staff of 1,200 Quicken Loans IT professionals can work individually or as a team on any personal project or idea they want, even those not related to the Quicken Loans business.

As a digital leader, He fervently believes in people. She is a relentless champion of the Quicken Loans' culture, personally embodying the intent and supporting her people. Regarding innovation, she stresses, "If you are afraid to make the mistake, you will never actually be creative and never think outside the box. Don't be afraid to fail."[10] Why go to these lengths? He believes in creating the conditions that attract digitally savvy talent and ideas, and then unleashing them in a way that drives amazing results on a sustained basis and has a tangible impact to the business.

It is one thing to be able to identify an attractive target culture such as that of Quicken Loans, but it's another story to transform an existing entrenched culture. Changing culture is no trivial matter. Let's look at a company that, in its 130-year history, has survived the Great Depression, nineteen recessions, and every major marketplace trend of the last thirteen decades.

Digital-Era Cultural Reset at GE

"Each major marketplace disruption calls for a reset of culture," Raghu Krishnamoorthy, GE's chief learning officer, explained. "Even though it is hard to re-create for the new context, if you don't you will not have the ability to survive. Our culture drives our longevity, and we don't hesitate to change it so we are contemporary and contextual to the current time."[11]

Krishnamoorthy believes that resetting culture is one of the most important skills the organization possesses, noting that GE has done it several times in the past, and will continue in the future. "This process doesn't stop. We'll constantly need to evolve to be relevant in the marketplace. Now is an exciting time because we are rebirthing the organization through a new digital lens," Krishnamoorthy said.[12]

Staying relevant to the current marketplace demands is crucial. While nobody reading this book would likely disagree, far fewer have the conviction and capability to transform culture to the needed degree or at the needed pace. By adeptly infusing such a cultural shift, GE seeks to make itself attractive to the best talent in the key areas of software and analytics that enable their Industrial Internet strategy.

For the "how" of transforming the company and building the needed digital muscle, GE is taking a multipart approach. First, it rolled out a technical tool kit called FastWorks, which leverages a mentality similar to that used by Silicon Valley or start-ups to address a set of key challenges: How do we experiment? How do we launch? How do we learn? How do we work in real time with our customers? But Krishnamoorthy is aware that a technical tool kit alone will not help if the organization doesn't have the cultural framework, particularly important for people who have been governed by Six Sigma and other past approaches that have been successful. If leaders are to pivot their mind-sets, they also need to change their frame of thinking to one more suited to the demands of today's digital-era marketplace.

To help leaders change their mind-sets, GE had to create a new cultural template that demands new ways of behaving. "We even called our new cultural orientation 'the GE Beliefs' to ensure that people changed their frame of thinking to the new way," Krishnamoorthy said. The GE Beliefs are: customers determine our success; stay lean to go fast; learn and adapt to win; empower and inspire each other; and deliver results in an uncertain world.[13] They reflect a renewed emphasis on acceleration, agility, and customer focus. "Interestingly, the GE Beliefs were crowdsourced from our employees for the first time—an attempt to drive a culture that the employees wanted to see."[14]

Krishnamoorthy recognized that to be a market leader, GE needed to adapt to a digital-era relevant culture internally faster than the external pace of change. But culture alone is not enough. As digital trends blur boundaries at every level, leaders and organizations need to remap internal structures and relationships, transform their relationships with customers and partners, and at times redefine the industry boundaries themselves.

Stepping Up As a Digital-Era Cartographer

As technology tipping points unleash waves of disruption, boundaries are in a state of flux, blurring, morphing, and mutating. This phenomenon occurs whether the boundary is between the physical and digital worlds, across value chains and ecosystems, or among traditional industry demarcation lines. In this shifting landscape, leaders must be flexible and open to change at their core, including the fundamental perspectives and mental models (maps) of how they view and understand the world.

Those digital leaders most adept at exploiting the disruption are not only open to changed perspectives but see through the fog to new opportunity spaces. They constantly strive to understand the new and ever-morphing contours at the confluence of digital and physical worlds. They seek to map and understand the new competitive terrain in ways that can help successful navigation. And in the most advanced cases, they remap this new, more virtual and malleable space in ways that place their enterprise at the center, or at key ports, hubs, or intersections where they can create more value or better serve their citizens. In a sense, they are the cartographers of the digital era.

To understand the relevance of mapmaking to today's leaders, consider the earliest cartographer, Anaximander, who was born in the city of Ionia (in modern-day Turkey) in 610 BC. He has been credited with the first attempt to map the known world.[15]

As an early proponent of science, and like many thinkers of the period, Anaximander explored and drew from many disciplines,

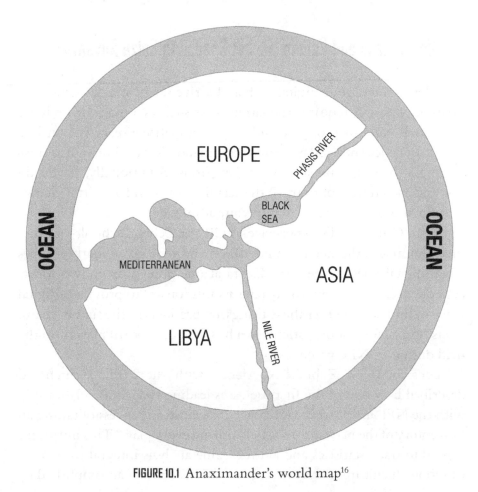

FIGURE 10.1 Anaximander's world map[16]

including as astronomy, physics, and philosophy. His map represented the ancient Greek understanding of the known inhabited world. But why go to the lengths of drawing such a map? Most likely, it was intended to improve trade routes in the region, or possibly to use as a tool to convince the Ionian city-states to join the federation and so strengthen its defenses against the hostile threats of the time.

Of course, cartography has come a long way since Anaximander's time. We use maps, models, and simulations to understand, navigate, and optimize the many layers of our world. And when disruption and associated discovery abounds, being a cartographer of sorts has great advantages to you as a digital leader. Let's consider how, by starting outside–in.

Understand and Remap Market Spaces to Seize Advantage

In order to travel your digital path and arrive safely at a desirable destination, you will require navigation tools such as a map. But relying on an old-world map of your industry's competitive space is a bit like navigating a journey today using Anaximander's world map. It is misleading at best, and possibly very dangerous. Additionally, if you do not understand the contours of the terrain, you will have little chance to influence, shape, or remap it to your advantage.

Dean Crutchfield's experience as CIO at Zebra Technologies further illuminates the need to understand and remap the market spaces when digital goes to the core. Zebra at one point was known for its bar code technology, but today cites its mission as "to provide a digital voice to things," whether those things are products in the supply chain, assets on a factory floor, patients in a hospital, or football players on the field during an NFL game.

Let's focus on Zebra's experience with the NFL. Crutchfield described how one of the first use cases leading to Zebra's relationship with the NFL involved automation of the existing process of taking an "inventory of the players on the field during every play." This inventory is used to track statistics and aid the game analysis integral to American football culture. Player inventory was historically accomplished by taking pictures before and during game plays, then using a manual process to derive the data. By instrumenting the players—"providing them a digital voice"—the process can now be accomplished automatically via sensors and algorithms.

Once players had a digital voice, the resolution revolution opened up new opportunity spaces. For example, coaches can leverage the rich data to analyze performance faster, noting successful versus unsuccessful plays. This enabled the creation of new forms of adjacent business and ecosystem partners, including software companies that create new types of coaching applications and gaming companies that create new fantasy games based on the data. In another example, broadcasters can embellish the plays or provide personalized digital services such as isolating a player. And it's now possible to create new fan experience apps that blur the physical reality of the game with digital avatar–embellished representations.

Drawing on a combination of technology savvy and business acumen as a natural on-ramp, Crutchfield helps Zebra's executive team remap these emerging market spaces, which they are in part creating by bringing a digital voice to things. He reflected that, "Initially, we explored playing a broader role in the ecosystem such as fan apps and other areas. But for now we are focused on creating markets and having strategic partnerships to handle the adjacency opportunities. Being able to define and create a market is a good position to be in."[17]

Just as Crutchfield does, many digital leaders navigate the shifting contours of new digital market space terrains. At a minimum, they instinctively seek to understand these new competitive spaces so they can find the most natural paths and avoid unnecessarily harsh territory. Whenever possible, they seek to influence or remap the space and strive for the competitive high ground and natural opportunities.

Recall how Arvind Gupta at the BJP played a role in remapping the contours of the Indian election campaign to influence outcomes via analytics, social, mobile, digital marketing, and even 3D holograms. Or how Bill Ruh leveraged advanced analytics to provide GE a way to redraw the contours of large-scale industrial markets via services and business outcomes, rather than merely selling turbines and aircraft engines. Or how Klas Bendrik at Volvo Cars discovered new customer value via the Roam service, remapping the delivery process at the intersection of the connected car platform, e-commerce, and transportation. And returning to our chapter 1 opening story, recall how Eric Babolat remapped tennis with his digital racquet all the way to the rule book. All are examples of digital-era cartographers, each looking to pioneer and remap the terrain in their particular competitive market spaces to gain advantage.

Remap "Inside Spaces" to Deliver Results

External marketplace disruptions necessitate an internal response, one in which digital leaders once again benefit from thinking like modern-day cartographers. This internal remapping enables the digital competencies described in chapter 7 to deliver results at the market speed demanded by the new competitive landscape.

Ford CEO Mark Fields described this relationship as starting outside—in: "Our ecosystem has widened beyond traditional automotive. The 'Internet of Things,' such as cities, other vehicles, infrastructure, and customer networks, all play an important role in the future of our industry." Explaining the resulting internal implications, he said, "We need to leverage our entire team to develop solutions to meet changing customer needs, create an industry leadership position, and, ultimately, change the way the world moves. So, we are creating cross-functional teams that span our enterprise and include collaborations with external partners to accelerate our work in connectivity, mobility, autonomous vehicles, the customer experience, and data and analytics—all the elements of our Ford Smart Mobility plan."[18] Fields's insight highlighted a key point, particularly pertinent for leaders in traditional enterprises—the need to span boundaries and deliver new capabilities cross functionally across the enterprise and beyond.

Ford's CIO Marcy Klevorn gave us an example of how Ford spans internal functions and remaps the way results are achieved across the enterprise. Klevorn and her team regularly champion innovation, increasingly focused at the blurring boundary between the car and digital. In the "Connected Vehicle Challenge," IT partnered with colleagues in product development and challenged the entire cross-functional Ford workforce to demonstrate how data from the connected vehicle could be shaped into new ideas that add value to the business and improve customer experience.

Teams had two weeks to come up with ideas, three weeks to explore the new technologies, and just seven days to analyze billions of vehicle events gathered from more than one hundred connected vehicles. In the end, forty-six teams across the world completed the challenge. Klevorn was delighted with the result: "An enthusiastic and energized cross-functional workforce focused on creating innovative solutions to key business challenges. The team illuminated several new business opportunities that are moving into production, all based on analyzing the connected vehicle data set."[19]

Returning to Madrid, Marco Bressan at BBVA also acted as a cartographer and, with his peers, remapped internal spaces to deliver and realize value from new data-centric capabilities. As Bressan's team of data scientists discovered new opportunities, they remapped the paths to market most suited to the contours of the opportunity. For example, where the new capability is for the core bank, such as the enhanced credit-scoring system, the optimal path is for the data and analytics unit to provide the data and the algorithm, then for the bank's internal units to incorporate it into their systems. When the innovation creates a completely new product or service, particularly if it's outside the bank's core financial services domain, experience showed that an alternative path was needed. In this case, the group partnered with an "internal ventures" entity (also part of BBVA Digital Bank) that had the competencies to productize and take the idea to market. In a third case, when neither part of the bank had sufficient interest in the idea, Bressan's team might partner in creative ways with start-ups or entrepreneurs, such as those that surfaced via the data innovation challenge discussed earlier in the chapter.

Draw Talent and Shape the Landscape for Digital Success

Talent with the necessary digital skills is becoming a particularly precious commodity, and a leader's ability to attract people with skill sets that are in high demand will be a key determinate of his success. This is a highly human process! Many advanced digital leaders have a mind-set that they are personally the attractors of talent, and, as we explained in this chapter, are very committed to achieving this goal.

But delivering on the vast promise of digital is about more than just attracting talent—it also requires the mind-set, competencies, structures, and processes that naturally fit the contours of digital market-place demands. And there is no point in attracting talent if it cannot thrive. New people will need new "fit for digital purpose" spaces to operate. As the competitive terrain repeatedly morphs, leaders can play a key role as digital-era cartographers, remapping both internal and external spaces in ways that enable digital capability and marketplace advantage.

Actionable Takeaways

Become an attractor of the best digital talent and ideas. Creatively remake yourself and aspects of your world so you can be a "magnet" for the key skills and innovation you seek. Pull others toward you.

Define and radiate a compelling digital purpose. Be a mission maker, so that people can be part of something worthwhile that is much bigger than themselves. Tightly link your group's mission to your enterprise's core purpose.

Remaster and nurture a "fit for digital purpose" culture. Ensure that the pace and type of change internally match or exceed the changes occurring externally. Lead and model the new cultural values and behaviors.

Remap your world to fit the contours of digital business. Think of yourself as a digital-era cartographer. Remake both internal and external spaces in ways that enable digital capability execution and seize marketplace advantage.

APPENDIX

Digital Business Competencies and Cultural Capabilities

To avoid a long list in chapter 7, we've placed a number of the items that appear in figure 7.1 into this appendix. Please refer to chapter 7 for descriptions of the following:

Platform thinking
Beta experimentation
Maker skills
Design thinking
Data science
User centricity
Relative risk thinking

Holacracy

Holacracy is an organizational style designed with little or no hierarchy and few formally designated management roles. Instead, authority and decision making are distributed across self-organizing teams. The design purpose is not social egalitarianism in the workforce; rather, holacracy is a way that some leading-edge born-digital companies have been evolving to enable local empowerment and continuous self-adapting reorganization. The method has been used at Zappos (one of our interviews for this book) to allow the company to pursue a relentless focus on delighting customers. The method has been written about in *Holacracy: The New Management System for a Rapidly Changing World* by Brian J. Roberson (Henry Holt and Co., 2015).

Tech Cluster Location

In this feature of the modern global economy, industry sectors and talent pools tend to cluster in certain countries, cities, and districts. This is certainly true for high-tech digital skills. Clusters exist in Silicon Valley, Tel Aviv, Tokyo, Seoul, Amsterdam, London, and so on. Born-digital companies usually base themselves in an existing or emerging cluster location to easily access talent, supporting business services such as venture capital, and the "can do" leading-edge culture related to their core enterprise endeavor.

Extreme Talent

Fast-moving tech start-ups often use small, intense teams of very high-capability individuals to accelerate progress. In a bell-shaped normal distribution of speed, productivity, and effectiveness in a specialist professional population, the top 1 percent or 0.1 percent can sometimes outperform median performers by many times—as one commenter said to us "multiple 10x." Though this understanding is common in sports, it still eludes many conventional corporate management cultures, where managing large ostensibly "upper quartile" groups with standardized methodologies is the preferred approach.

Crowdsourcing

Many start-ups and born-digital companies treat the social Internet as a default sourcing method for a variety of resources. The "crowd"—people on the Internet who might be able to combine to help solve a problem—is a powerful way of generating ideas, funding, collaborative media, market insight, and more.

Geek Reverence

The caricature of the geeky ponytail-wearing techie, along with Dilbert and other simplifications, has too often allowed businesspeople in large corporations to deride the smart technical people they need most to advance their companies.

The same businesspeople who admire Jonathan Ive and Mark Zuckerberg are often shockingly dismissive of their own technical specialists. If you want to succeed in digital business, this double standard has to end. Dynamic tension will always be present between roles and disciplines, but in the end mutual professional respect is the hallmark of all great digital success stories.

Smart Machine First

At the heart of the tech companies that lead our age is a belief that machines can be made to do anything, and that as soon as it's possible they should. That belief enabled IBM to create a machine that could beat humans on the TV game show *Jeopardy*. The same technology is being used by MD Anderson Cancer Center to create an oncology expert advisor system that absorbs and organizes vast amounts of the knowledge of clinicians and researchers.[20]

If your company's first and only response to growth is "add people," you are not thinking digitally. A born-digital company will always ask if there is software that can do the work, or if it can be created.

Lean Start-Up/MVP

The often-repeated excuse that large traditional companies use for digital inaction is that they simply can't innovate or move at the pace of "born-digital" Silicon Valley start-ups. This smacks of complacency and capitulation. Management author Eric Ries was tired of hearing this well-worn refrain through the early 2000s so he decided to fix it. His book, *The Lean Startup*,[21] describes how to take a few of the common methods of Silicon Valley start-ups and transpose them into the large corporate context. His work has been so successful that, in our research, interviewees often mentioned "MVP" (minimum viable product) and "pivoting."

Insanely Great

Steve Jobs famously wanted to make products that were "insanely great." His personal example has become an inspiration to a generation of digital entrepreneurs. Delighting the customer to the extreme with the product and services experience, rather than relying heavily on marketing spend, has become a business approach that many try to emulate. One of the companies we interviewed for this book, Zappos, is a great example of this, with its "wow" customer service ethos.

Openness and Open Innovation

All digital businesses must be open to a greater or lesser extent. The level of openness may ebb and flow, but it is a prerequisite for success. Like it or not, your systems will probably be using open source software and your data scientists will be using some open data. Sometimes, harnessing the contributions of outsiders will be the only way to make progress at the pace you need to compete. You can't expect others to be open with you if you still have the closed and secretive mind-set of a traditional corporation.

Venturing

Born-digital businesses and the tech start-ups you are competing against are highly entrepreneurial and risk taking. They aim for very fast growth, and if they are publicly traded they usually offer investors the promise of capital growth rather than dividend yield returns. Their financial profile and risk-taking attitudes may be hard to match from within your low-growth, low-risk business. Creating separate new ventures or joint ventures might be a way to close that gap. Some of the big tech companies themselves find this necessary from time to time in order to move at the pace of a new start-up sector.

Cloud-Based Business

All that data coming out of things and being accessed by businesses needs to "live" somewhere, and because of the scale of the data, that somewhere has to be a pretty big place. The cloud is increasingly recognized as a "place" to do business and to grow business, rather than as a style of computing that reduces the IT department's server bill.

Business Model Experimentation

Razorblade, freemium, long-tail, and pay-as-you-go are examples of business models. In digital business, your leadership team will need to be regularly experimenting with business model ideas. Fluency in business models is a hallmark of born-digital companies, which often try several and switch models more than once.

Social Analytics

Many of today's strongest born-digital businesses grew up with the social Internet. For them, it is natural to be connected with talent pools, suppliers, and customers in this way. It is also the way they examine market behaviors. Analysis of tweets, Facebook status updates, and LinkedIn relationships helps them understand how customers are developing and relaying thoughts about the company and its products. If your company still relies only on old research techniques like focus groups, it is missing out on a powerful source of insight.

A/B Testing

Born-digital companies often have the discipline of testing every idea with a measured response and letting the data decide what works and what doesn't. They use technology to apply a champion/challenger competition that pits each new innovation against the old method. Traditional firms have often allowed too much subjective "expert" and committee opinion to intervene in their research. Fortunately, the Internet allows a firm to test an idea quickly and for very little cost. Define the test, measure the result, and let the decision become automatic.

Tiny Sourcing

Large companies often source what they need from other large companies. This has been especially true in the context of traditional IT. However, to move quickly and innovatively—to lead digital change in an industry—you must be prepared and able to work with very small firms, including those with only three or four employees. Some of the most important digital breakthroughs were possible by sourcing from tiny pockets of niche talent at freelancer scale.

Coopetition

Tech sector companies are expert at operating in a world where this week's competitor becomes next week's supplier, customer, or both. They develop a deep natural culture of cooperation and competition—or coopetition. They have the mechanisms and internal dividing walls to manage the tensions and duality. For example, Apple and Samsung compete fiercely for market share in consumer mobile devices. However, Apple has often relied on Samsung to provide key components for its own machines..

Gamification

Gamification is the use of game mechanics and experience design to digitally engage and motivate people to achieve their goals. It has emerged as a way to gain an edge by engaging people on an emotional level. It's a powerful method for pulling together the different elements of your digital offer and getting people to use them coherently in their lives. Our colleague Brian Burke, vice president, detailed the player-centric design process in his book *Gamify: How Gamification Motivates People to Do Extraordinary Things* (Bibliomotion, 2014).[22]

Mission Matters

Elon Musk's Tesla Motors was "founded in 2003 by a group of engineers in Silicon Valley who wanted to prove that electric cars could be better than gasoline-powered cars."[23] Google's mission is "to organize the world's information and make it universally accessible and useful."[24] The leaders of the high-tech firms are commonly driven by a determination to achieve truly great things in their chosen fields. If they come into direct competition with you through the blurring boundaries of digital business, will your people be equally motivated?

Digital Innovation Centers

Digital innovation centers can be created wherever there is a tech cluster and talent to draw from. California, in particular, has seen a wave of corporate digital innovation center openings over the last few years, especially in the Silicon Valley and San Francisco Bay areas. Examples include MacDonald's, Ford, GE, Westfield, Visa, Capital One, Target, Wells Fargo, Walmart, UNICEF, Bayer, BNY Mellon, Volkswagen, Honda, and Nestlé. Organizations go there for the supporting infrastructure, culture, and talent. They benefit from positioning themselves alongside major technology companies like Google and Apple and among the myriad start-ups and VCs that set a driving energy and pace.

Agile Software Development

Digital development is usually evolutionary and exploratory. Often, ideas become prototypes, prototypes are tested, reactions refine them, and progress is made. The traditional software development methods assumed that a perfect design could be conceived and written down first, a bit like the design of a bridge or a building. However, that is rarely the way breakthrough software innovation happens. Instead, your teams need strong capability in agile project methods such as Scrum and Kanban, together with development techniques such as test-driven development and extreme programming.

NOTES

Chapter 1

1. Eric Babolat, interview with author Mark Raskino, December 16, 2014.
2. Babolat interview.
3. International Tennis Federation Rule 31, accessed March 8, 2015, http://www.itftennis.com/technical/publications/rules/player-analysis-technology/overview.aspx.
4. Tennis Industry Association dashboard, accessed March 8, 2015, http://www.tennisindustry.org/cms/index.cfm/research/industry-dashboard/?.
5. First Research, "Sporting Goods Stores Industry Profile," Hoover's Inc., accessed March 8, 2015, http://www.firstresearch.com/Industry-Research/Sporting-Goods-Stores.html.
6. Dave Bone, "String Selector 2014," *Tennis Industry* magazine, January 2014, accessed March 8, 2015, http://www.tennisindustrymag.com/articles/2014/01/3_string_selector_2014.html.
7. *The 2014 Gartner CEO and Senior Executive Survey: 'Risk-On' Attitudes Will Accelerate Digital Business*, Mark Raskino, April 9, 2014, http://www.gartner.com/document/2704918.
8. *Gartner 2015 CEO Survey: Committing to Digital,* Mark Raskino, April 10, 2015.
9. Gartner, "Digital" glossary definition, accessed March 8, 2015, http://www.gartner.com/it-glossary/digital.
10. *Gartner 2014 CIO Agenda Report,* http://www.gartner.com/document/2643016.
11. Gartner "Digital Business" glossary definition, accessed May 26, 2015, http://www.gartner.com/it-glossary/digital-business/.
12. *Wikipedia*, "Amazon Kindle," accessed March 8, 2015, http://en.wikipedia.org/wiki/Amazon_Kindle.

13. Katie Allen, "Amazon e-Book Sales Overtake Print for the First Time," *Guardian,* December 28, 2009. http://www.theguardian.com/business/2009/dec/28/amazon-ebook-kindle-sales-surge.

14. Samuel Gibbs, "Apple Agrees to Pay $450m Settlement in eBook Price Fixing Case," *Guardian,* July 16, 2014, http://www.theguardian.com/technology/2014/jul/16/apple-agrees-settlement-ebook-price-fixing; Brian X. Chen and Nicole Perlroth, "Settlement in Apple Case Over E-Books Is Approved," *New York Times,* November 21, 2014, http://www.nytimes.com/2014/11/22/technology/judge-approves-450-million-settlement-in-apple-e-book-case.html.

15. *Wikipedia,* "Hon Lik," accessed March 8, 2015, http://en.wikipedia.org/wiki/Hon_Lik.

16. Andrew Goodman, "E-Cigarettes Are Smoking Hot—Four Ways to Invest in Them," *Forbes,* May 12, 2013, http://www.forbes.com/sites/agoodman/2013/12/05/e-cigarettes-are-smoking-hot-4-ways-to-approach-them/.

17. Bonnie Herzog (senior analyst), "U.S. Tobacco Trends: Disruptive Innovation Should Drive Outsized Growth," Wells Fargo Securities, March 20, 2014, accessed via ecita.org.uk, May 25, 2015, http://www.ecita.org.uk/sites/default/files/Wells%20Fargo%20E-Cig%20Summit%20Presentation%20-%20Dallas%20March%202014.pdf.

18. Jeffrey Immelt, GE Minds & Machines Conference Keynote Speech, New York, October 9, 2014, https://www.youtube.com/watch?v=UUw4SfXzMrw.

19. "End of an Era—Why General Electric Has Sold Off Its Domestic-Appliances Division," *Economist,* September 8, 2014, http://www.economist.com/news/business-and-finance/21616209-end-era.

20. Michael J. De La Merced, "GE Files to Spin Off Retail Finance Unit," *New York Times,* March 13, 2014, http://dealbook.nytimes.com/2014/03/13/g-e-files-to-spin-off-retail-finance-unit/?_r=0.

21. William Ruh, telephone interview with authors, January 15, 2015.

22. William Ruh, telephone interview with authors, June 4, 2014.

23. Ruh interview, June 4, 2014.

24. Alfonso Velosa et al., "Gartner Predicts 2015: The Internet of Things," December 30, 2014, http://www.gartner.com/document/2952822.

25. "Internet World Stats," accessed May 25, 2015, http://www.internetworldstats.com/stats.htm.

26. Eric Babolat and Thomas Orton, e-mail to Mark Raskino, February 27, 2015.

27. Tom Perrotta, "The Racket of the Future," *Wall Street Journal,* June 2, 2012, http://www.wsj.com/articles/SB10001424052702303674004577434350145781454.

Chapter 2

1. Mark Fields (CEO, Ford Motor Company), keynote address, Consumer Electronics Show, Las Vegas, Nevada, January 2015, https://www.youtube.com/watch?v=lXjJ4pF0d7c.

2. Mark Fields (CEO, Ford Motor Company.), in e-mail interview with authors, March 18, 2015.

3. Ford, press release reporting 2015 CES speech, January 16, 2015, https://media.ford.com/content/fordmedia/fna/us/en/news/2015/01/06/ford-at-ces-announces-smart-mobility-plan.html.

4. Mark Fields (CEO, Ford Motor Company), in e-mail interview with authors, March 18, 2015.

5. Raj Nair (CTO Product Development, Ford Motor Company), Consumer Electronics Show Keynote, January 2015, http://youtu.be/lXjJ4pF0d7c.

6. Jeffrey Immelt, interview by Geoff Elliott, transcript published in the *Australian*, March 20, 2013, accessed March 8, 2015, http://www.theaustralian.com.au/business/transcript-jeff-immelt-interview/story-e6frg8zx-1226601891721.

7. Aviva Drive app, http://www.aviva.co.uk/drive/.

8. WeatherSignal.com, http://weathersignal.com/.

9. Moore's law is more specifically the observation that, over the history of computing hardware, the number of transistors in a dense integrated circuit has doubled approximately every two years. These circuits include microprocessors, memory, some sensors, and screen technologies. Moore's law also acts as a goal and challenge to the IT industry, to maintain the pace of advancement.

10. Murray Kessler, video interview by ecigadvanced.com, recorded April 2012, accessed via YouTube March 8, 2015, https://www.youtube.com/watch?v=urjs_pI5k_o&feature=youtu.be.

11. Vuse website, accessed March 8, 2015, https://vusevapor.com/.

12. Adam Sherwin, "'Smart' e-Cigarette Can Keep Track of Every Puff," *Independent*, October 13, 2014, accessed March 8, 2015, http://www.independent.co.uk/life-style/health-and-families/health-news/smart-ecigarette-can-keep-track-of-every-puff-9792178.html.

13. Proteus Digital Health website, accessed March 8, 2015, http://www.proteus.com/technology/digital-health-feedback-system.

14. Dana Daisy, interview by Gartner Research, November 12, 2013, http://www.gartner.com/document/2647515.

15. Arjen Dorland (EVP of technical and competitive IT, Shell), telephone interview with authors, September 25, 2014.

16. Volvo Sensus Connect website, accessed July 7, 2015, http://www.volvocars.com/intl/services/apps-and-services/sensus-connect.

17. Atif Rafiq (CDO, McDonald's), telephone interview with authors, September 26, 2014; Brian Crecente, "McDonald's Rolls Out 1.5 Billion Fry Boxes for Augmented-Reality World Cup Video Game," Polygon.com, June 30, 2014, accessed March 8, 2015, http://www.polygon.com/2014/6/30/5856816 /fifa-world-cup-augmented-reality-game.

18. The distinction between "bit" and "atom" industries was first made by Nicholas Negroponte in *Being Digital,* published in 1995, http://en.wikipedia .org/wiki/Being_Digital.

19. Steve Perry (chief digital officer of Visa Europe), interview with authors, August 14, 2014.

Chapter 3

1. "Waryong Park," Visit Korea page of the Korea Tourism Organization, accessed May 31, 2015, http://english.visitkorea.or.kr/enu/SI/SI_EN_3_1_1_1.jsp?cid =1061789.

2. Dr. Hee Hwang (chief information officer and chief medical officer, Seoul National University Bundang Hospital), telephone interview with authors, January 20, 2015.

3. Akamai State of the Internet Report, 2014, http://content.akamai.com /PG1183-StateoftheInternet.html.

4. "2013 Survey on Internet Usage," Korea Internet & Security Agency, 2013, http://isis.kisa.or.kr/eng/.

5. Bob Howard, "Insurer Stops 'Pay as You Drive,'" BBC News, June 14, 2008, accessed March 9, 2015, http://news.bbc.co.uk/1/hi/programmes/ moneybox/7453546.stm.

6. Aviva (formerly Norwich Union), press releases announcing pay-as-you -drive insurance, accessed March 9, 2015, http://www.aviva.co.uk/media -centre/story/2840/norwich-union-launches-innovative-pay-as-you-drive/, http://www.aviva.co.uk/media-centre/story/2586/norwich-union-and -trafficmaster-sign-deal-for-blac/, http://www.aviva.co.uk/media-centre/story/ 1386/norwich-union-appoints-ibm-and-orange-for-pay-as-y/.

7. "Norwich Union Axes "Pay as You Drive" Scheme," *Motor Trader,* June 18, 2008, accessed March 9, 2015, http://www.motortrader.com/general-news /norwich-union-axes-pay-as-you-drive-scheme/.

8. *Korea Internet Security Agency Internet Statistics Report 2013,* accessed March 9, 2015, http://isis.kisa.or.kr/eng/.

9. Dr. Hee Hwang, telephone interview with authors, January 20, 2015.

10. Hwang interview.

11. Aviva, press release introducing the Aviva Drive app, November 26, 2012, accessed March 9, 2015, http://www.aviva.com/media/news/item/uk-aviva -launches-its-new-aviva-drive-app-17048/.

12. Aviva, press release regarding the success of the Aviva Drive app, August 4, 2014, accessed March 9, 2015, http://www.aviva.com/media/news/item/uk-aviva-drive-app-drives-down-the-cost-of-car-insurance-by-101-for-safer-drivers-17332/.

13. *Wikipedia*, "Boo.com," accessed March 9, 2015, http://en.wikipedia.org/wiki/Boo.com.

14. Ernst Malmsten, Erik Portanger, and Charles Drazin, *Boo Hoo: A Dot.com Story from Concept to Catastrophe* (Random House UK, New Ed edition, 2002).

15. Grace Jessup, "Fashion Chains H&M and Zara Launch Online Operations," *Guardian*, August 9, 2010, http://www.theguardian.com/business/2010/aug/09/zara-fashion-retail-industry.

16. Michael Pastore, "Women Maintain Lead in Internet Use," ClickZ, June 18, 2001, http://www.clickz.com/clickz/news/1714809/women-maintain-lead-internet-use.

17. Tory Burch for Fitbit website, accessed May 31, 2015, http://www.fitbit.com/uk/toryburch#1.

18. Mike Giresi (CIO, Tory Burch), telephone interview with authors, February 1, 2015.

19. *Wikipedia*, "William Gibson," accessed June 1, 2015, http://en.wikiquote.org/wiki/William_Gibson.

20. John Peretiatko (senior director corporate applications, Zappos), telephone interview with authors, January 21, 2015, and meeting with authors at Zappos, May 27–28, 2015.

21. Eric Babolat, interview with authors, December 16, 2014.

22. Marcus Barnes, "What's Bin Going On? New Network on the Streets of London Broadcasts News to City Workers via Recycling Bins," *Daily Mail*, January 27, 2012, http://www.dailymail.co.uk/news/article-2092367/London-broadcasts-news-City-workers-recycling-bins.html.

23. James Vincent, "London's Bins Are Tracking Your Smartphone," *Independent*, August 9, 2013, http://www.independent.co.uk/life-style/gadgets-and-tech/news/updated-londons-bins-are-tracking-your-smartphone-8754924.html.

24. Joe Miller, "City of London Calls Halt to Smartphone Tracking Bins," BBC News, August 12, 2013, http://www.bbc.co.uk/news/technology-23665490.

25. Christine Negroni, "Tracking Your Wi-Fi Trail," *New York Times*, March 21, 2011, http://www.nytimes.com/2011/03/22/business/22airport.html?_r=0.

26. Mark Raskino, "Copenhagen Airport Uses Location-Based Technology for Competitive Advantage," Gartner Research, November 15, 2011, https://www.gartner.com/doc/1849315/copenhagen-airport-uses-locationbased-technology.

27. Roger Liew (senior vice president and CTO, Orbitz), telephone interview with authors, January 29, 2015.

28. Mike Bracken (executive director of digital, U.K. Government Cabinet Office), interview with authors, August 26, 2014.

29. Brad Stone, "DJI's Drone Is Simple Enough for Anyone to Use," Bloomberg, May 15, 2014, http://www.bloomberg.com/bw/articles/2014-05-15/dji-inno vations-drone-is-simple-enough-for-anyone-to-use.

30. Michael Patrick Perry, director of communication at DJI, in "This is the most amazing drone we've seen yet," the *Verge*, November 12, 2014, interview quote from 4:32 to 4:58 in video accessed via YouTube, May 31, 2015, www.you tube.com/watch?v=XdlmoLAbbiQ

31. Arvind Gupta (innovation evangelist, information and technology head, Bharatiya Janata Party), telephone interview with authors, February 17, 2015.

32. David Duffy (CEO, AIB) telephone interview with authors, November 3, 2014.

33. Rory Cellan-Jones, "Google Glass Sales Halted but Firm Says Kit Is Not Dead," BBC News, January 15, 2015, http://www.bbc.co.uk/news/technology -30831128.

34. Nick Bilton, "Why Google Glass Broke," *New York Times,* February 4, 2015, http://www.nytimes.com/2015/02/05/style/why-google-glass-broke.htm.

35. "Google to 'Start Again' with Glass Project," BBC News, February 6, 2015, http://www.bbc.co.uk/news/technology-31164840.

36. Oakley Airwave product website, accessed May 31, 2015, http://www.oakley .com/en/collection/airwave.

Chapter 4

1. Maurice Levy (CEO, Publicis Groupe), interview with authors, December 9, 2014.

2. Linda Kerstin, "7 Key Insights by Maurice Lévy, Chairman and CEO of Publicis Groupe," *Berlin School of Creative Leadership* blog, accessed May 31, 2015, http://www.berlin-school.com/news-media/blogs/blogentry/lunch -talk-with-maurice-levy-chairman-and-ceo-of-publicis-groupe-pioneering -communication-on-beh/.

3. Adam Thomson, "Maurice Lévy Tries to Pick Up Publicis After Failed Deal with Omnicom," *Financial Times,* December 14, 2014, http://www.ft.com/ intl/cms/s/0/377f7054-81ef-11e4-b9d0-00144feabdc0.html#axzz3TzttJU4G.

4. "Autonomous Driving Renault NEXT TWO, for an Affordable, Hypercon-nected Mobile Lifestyle," Renault Press Kit, February 6, 2014, http://media .renault.com/download/media/specialfile/54698_1_5.aspx.

5. Roger Liew (CTO, Orbitz), telephone interview with authors, January 29, 2015.

6. Klas Bendrik (SVP and CIO Volvo Cars), telephone interview with Graham Waller and Dave Aron, May 5, 2014.

7. Eric Babolat, interview with author Mark Raskino, December 16, 2014.

8. Roger Liew (CTO, Orbitz), telephone interview with authors, January 29, 2015.

9. David Duffy (CEO, Allied Irish Banks), telephone interview with authors, November 3, 2014.

10. Francisco González, "Banks Need to Take on Amazon and Google or Die," *Financial Times,* December 2, 2013, http://www.ft.com/cms/s/0/bc70c9fe -4e1d-11e3-8fa5-00144feabdc0.html.

11. Maurice Levy (CEO, Publicis Groupe), interview with authors, December 9, 2014.

12. Nestlé BabyNes website, accessed May 31, 2015, http://www.babynes.com/ ch-fr/services/application-iphone-bebe-nutrition.

13. Proteus Digital Health website, accessed May 31, 2015, http://www.proteus .com/.

14. Doug McMillon, "Picking Up the Pace of Change for the Customer," Walmart News & Views Executive Viewpoints, June 6, 2014, http://news.walmart.com/ executive-viewpoints/picking-up-the-pace-of-change-for-the-customer.

15. "Amazon Customers Become Designers with New 3D Printed Products Store Offering Customizable Fashion Accessories, Toys, Home Décor and More," Business Wire, July 28, 2014, http://www.businesswire.com/news/home/2014 0728005144/en/Amazon-Customers-Designers-3D-Printed-Products-Store.

16. Andrew S. Grove, *Only the Paranoid Survive* (Profile Books, New Ed edition, 1998).

17. Maurice Levy (CEO, Publicis Groupe), interview with authors, December 9, 2014.

18. Levy interview.

19. Tobias Buck, "BBVA Buys US Digital Bank Simple to Increase Online Offering," *Financial Times,* February 20, 2014, http://www.ft.com/intl/cms/s/0/ f8c9e086-9a3d-11e3-a407-00144feab7de.html; "Monsanto Acquires Climate Corporation," Monsanto website, accessed May 31, 2015, http://www.mon santo.com/features/pages/monsanto-acquires-the-climate-corporation .aspx; Minsi Chung, "Under Armour Buying MapMyFitness in $150 Million Deal," Bloomberg, November 14, 2013, http://www.bloomberg.com/news/ articles/2013-11-14/under-armour-to-buy-fitness-technology-company-for -150-million.

20. "About: Acquisitions," WalmartLabs website, accessed May 31, 2015, http:// www.walmartlabs.com/about/acquisitions/.

21. Monte Burke, "Under Armour, with First-Ever Acquisition, Enters the World of Software," *Forbes,* November 14, 2013, http://www.forbes.com/sites/ monteburke/2013/11/14/under-armour-with-first-ever-acquisition-enters -the-world-of-software/.

22. Burke, "Under Armour, with First-Ever Acquisition."

23. Burke, "Under Armour, with First-Ever Acquisition."

24. Marcy Klevorn (CIO, Ford Motor Company), meeting with author February 19, 2015, and e-mail interview with authors, May 6, 2015.

25. Cliff Saran, "Executive Interview: GE Software Chief Bill Ruh on Value of an Industrial Cloud," *Computer Weekly,* March 6, 2015, http://www.computer weekly.com/news/2240241843/Executive-interview-GEs-software-chief -Bill-Ruh-on-value-of-an-industrial-cloud.

26. "GE to Open Up Predix Industrial Internet Platform to All Users," Business Wire, October 9, 2014, http://www.businesswire.com/news/home/2014100 9005691/en/GE-Open-Predix-Industrial-Internet-Platform-Users# .VQCSvPmsV8E.

27. "Everything You Always Wanted to Know About Predix, but Were Afraid to Ask," GE Reports, October 9, 2014, http://www.gereports.com/post /99494485070/everything-you-always-wanted-to-know-about-predix.

28. Cliff Saran, "Executive Interview: GE Software Chief Bill Ruh on Value of an Industrial Cloud," *Computer Weekly,* March 6, 2015, http://www.comput erweekly.com/news/2240241843/Executive-interview-GEs-software-chief -Bill-Ruh-on-value-of-an-industrial-cloud.

29. Mark Ballard, "Pull Out and Keep Our Guide to UK Gov IT Failures," *Computer Weekly,* May 31, 2013, http://www.computerweekly.com/blogs/ public-sector/2013/05/pull-out-and-keepyour-guide-to.html.

30. "Mike Bracken Appointed as Government's Director of Digital," Wired.co.uk, May 20, 2011, http://www.wired.co.uk/news/archive/2011-05/20/mike -bracken-digital-director.

31. Steve Perry (chief digital officer Visa Europe), interview with authors, August 14, 2014.

Chapter 5

1. Steve Perry (CDO, Visa Europe), interview with authors, August 14, 2014.

2. Perry interview.

3. Perry interview.

6. Neil Munshi, "New McDonald's Chief Faces Kitchen Heat," *Financial Times,* January 29, 2015, http://www.ft.com/cms/s/0/07b690a0-a765-11e4-b6bd -00144feab7de.html#axzz3bk7NnVKk.

7. Andria Cheng, "Why Steve Easterbrook Is McDonald's Man," *MarketWatch,* January 30, 2015, http://www.marketwatch.com/story/why-steve-easterbrook -is-mcdonalds-man-2015-01-29.

8. Jim Sappington (EVP, operations and technology systems, McDonald's) and Atif Rafiq (EVP and chief digital officer, McDonald's), telephone interview with authors, September 26, 2014.

9. Sappington and Rafiq interview.
10. Sappington and Rafiq interview.
11. Sappington and Rafiq interview.
12. Eric Babolat (CEO, Babolat), interview with authors, December 16, 2014.
13. Mary Mesaglio and Simon Mingay, "Bimodal IT: How to Be Digitally Agile Without Making a Mess," Gartner Research, July 15, 2014, http://www .gartner.com/document/code/268866.
14. Airwave product page, Oakley website, accessed June 1, 2015, http://www .oakley.com/en/collection/airwave.
15. Manuela Mesco, "Italian Eyewear Maker Luxottica Working on New Version of Google Glass, CEO Says," *Wall Street Journal,* April 24, 2015, http://blogs.wsj .com/digits/2015/04/24/italian-eyewear-maker-luxottica-working-on-new -version-of-google-glass-ceo-says/.
16. Ken Daly (CEO, NACD), telephone interview with authors, September 28, 2014.
17. David Duffy (CEO, AIB), telephone interview with authors, November 3, 2014.
18. Mark Raskino, "CIOs Must Reappraise the Role of Chief Strategy Officers," Gartner Research, January 14, 2015, http://www.gartner.com/document /2963118.
19. Mark Fields (CEO, Ford), e-mail interview with authors, March 18, 2015.
20. Mark Raskino, *The 2014 Gartner CEO and Senior Executive Survey: "Risk-On" Attitudes Will Accelerate Digital Business,* April 9, 2014, http://www.gartner. com/document/2704918.
21. Klas Bendrik (VP and group CIO, Volvo Car Group), interview with authors, May 5, 2014.

Chapter 6

1. "Southeast Asia: India," CIA *World Factbook,* Central Intelligence Agency, 2014, accessed June 1, 2015, https://www.cia.gov/library/publications/the -world-factbook/geos/in.html.
2. "The Role of Digital in Winning an Election for the Bharatiya Janata Party of India," October 22, 2014, http://www.gartner.com/document/ 2883125.
3. Jason Burke, "Narendra Modi's Landslide Victory Shatters Congress's Grip on India," *Guardian,* May 16, 2014, http://www.theguardian.com/world/2014/ may/16/narendra-modi-victory-congress-india-election.
4. Arvind Gupta (innovation evangelist, information and technology head, Bharatiya Janata Party), interview with authors, February 17, 2015.
5. Gupta interview.
6. Gupta interview.

7. Dave Aron, Graham Waller, and Lee Weldon, "The Role of Digital in Winning an Election for the Bharatiya Janata Party of India," Gartner Research, October 22, 2014, http://www.gartner.com/document/2883125.

8. Raghu Krishnamoorthy (VP, executive development, and chief learning officer, GE), telephone interview with authors, March 9, 2015.

9. "What Is Singularity University?," Singularity University website, accessed June 1, 2015, http://singularityu.org/overview/.

10. Raghu Krishnamoorthy (VP, executive development, and chief learning officer, GE), telephone interview with authors, March 9, 2015.

11. Raghu Krishnamoorthy, "GE's Culture Challenge After Welch and Immelt," *Harvard Business Review*, January 26, 2015, https://hbr.org/2015/01/ges-culture-challenge-after-welch-and-immelt.

12. Maurice Levy (CEO, Publicis Groupe), interview with authors, Paris, December 9, 2014.

13. *Wikipedia,* "Quicken Loans," accessed June 1, 2015, http://en.wikipedia.org/wiki/Quicken_Loans.

14. "Quicken Loans Fast Facts," Quicken Loans website, accessed June 1, 2015, http://www.quickenloans.com/press-room/fast-facts/.

15. *J.D. Power Special Power Report: Quicken Loans,* 2014, J.D. Power website, accessed June 1, 2015, http://www.jdpower.com/microsites/quicken-loans-home.

16. *GE Annual Report 2013,* CEO letter to shareowners, GE website, accessed June 1, 2015, https://www.gesoftware.com/news-events/featured-stories/annual-report-highlights-industrial-internet-and-ge-predictivity-0.

17. "Digital by Default Service Standard," U.K. Government website, accessed June 1, 2015, https://www.gov.uk/service-manual/digital-by-default.

18. "NACD President and CEO Ken Daly Testifies Before Congress on Improving Dodd-Frank's Whistleblower Protections," PR Newswire, May 12, 2011, http://www.prnewswire.com/news-releases/nacd-president-and-ceo-ken-daly-testifies-before-congress-on-improving-dodd-franks-whistleblower-protections-121721908.html.

19. Ken Daly (CEO, NACD), telephone interview with authors, September 28, 2014.

20. Daly interview.

21. Daly interview.

22. Daly interview.

23. "Spencer Stuart U.S. Board Index 2014," accessed June 1, 2015, https://www.spencerstuart.com/research-and-insight/spencer-stuart-us-board-index-2014.

24. Ken Daly (CEO, NACD), telephone interview with authors, September 28, 2014.

25. Raghu Krishnamoorthy, "GE's Culture Challenge After Welch and Immelt," *Harvard Business Review*, January 26, 2015, https://hbr.org/2015/01/ges-culture -challenge-after-welch-and-immelt.

26. Michael J. De La Merced, "Eastman Kodak Files for Bankruptcy," *New York Times,* January 19, 2012, http://dealbook.nytimes.com/2012/01/19/eastman -kodak-files-for-bankruptcy.

27. Daniel J. Flynn, "Blockbuster Goes Bust," *American Spectator,* November 15, 2013, http://spectator.org/articles/56507/blockbuster-goes-bust.

28. Eric Platt, "SkyMall Bankruptcy Grounds Flying Yetis," *Financial Times,* January 23, 2015, http://on.ft.com/1BS8G0a.

29. Summarized from Mark Raskino and John Mahoney, "CIO New Year's Resolutions, 2015," Gartner Research, January 9, 2015, http://www.gartner.com/document/2959234.

30. A. Charles Thomas (chief data officer, Wells Fargo), telephone interview with authors, October 31, 2014.

31. Thomas interview.

32. Mark Raskino, *2015 CEO Survey: Committing to Digital,* April 10, 2015, http://www.gartner.com/document/3026817.

Chapter 7

1. Bill Ruh (VP, GE Software), telephone interview with authors, June 4, 2014.

2. Mike Bracken (executive director of digital, U.K. Government Cabinet Office), interview with authors, August 26, 2014.

3. Bracken interview.

4. Nicholas G. Carr, "IT Doesn't Matter," *Harvard Business Review,* May 2003, https://hbr.org/2003/05/it-doesnt-matter.

5. Mark Raskino, *2015 CEO Survey: Committing to Digital,* April 10, 2015, http://www.gartner.com/document/3026817.

6. Raskino, *2015 CEO Survey.*

7. Gordon Bock, Kimberley Carpenter, and Jo Ellen Davis, "Management's Newest Star, Meet the Chief Information Officer,", *Businessweek*, October 13, 1986.

8. Ruh interview.

9. Ruh interview.

10. Francisco González, CEO BBVA, video interview with Maria Bartiromo, Fox Business, October 10, 2014, accessed June 14, 2015, http://video.foxbusiness.com/v/3832487768001/bbva-ceo-there-is-no-option-but-being-digital/.

11. Marco Bressan (chairman and CEO, BBVA Data & Analytics), interview with authors, January 15, 2015.

12. Denise Clark (SVP, chief information officer, Estée Lauder), telephone interview with authors, September 11, 2014.

13. "Under Armour Opens First Digital Headquarters in Austin's Revitalized Seaholm Power Plant District," PR Newswire, March 11, 2015, http://www.prnewswire.com/news-releases/under-armour-opens-first-digital-headquarters-in-austins-revitalized-seaholm-power-plant-district-300048813.html.
14. Bressan interview.
15. Bressan interview
16. Atif Rafiq (chief digital officer, McDonald's Corporation), telephone interview with authors, September 26, 2014.
17. Russell Davies (director of strategy, U.K. Government Digital Service), interview with authors, September 26, 2014.
18. Aurélie Barbaux, "Insuffler un esprit 'makers' dans l'entreprise," L'usine nouvelle, May 1, 2014, http://www.usinenouvelle.com/article/insuffler-un-esprit-makers-dans-l-entreprise.N258482.
19. Steve Tobak, "Facebook's Mark Zuckerberg—Insights for Entrepreneurs," CBS Moneywatch, October 31, 2011, http://www.cbsnews.com/news/facebooks-mark-zuckerberg-insights-for-entrepreneurs/.

Chapter 8

1. Pete Goss, conversations with author and remarks at Gartner CIO Forum, May 23, 2012, Washington D.C.; Pete Goss personal website, http://www.petegoss.com/.
2. Pete Goss conversations and remarks at Gartner CIO Forum.
3. Mark Fields (CEO, Ford Motor Corporation), e-mail interview with authors, May 6, 2015.
4. Fields interview.
5. Fields interview.
6. Marcy Klevorn (CIO, Ford Motor Corporation), meeting with author, February 19, 2015, and e-mail interview with authors, May 6, 2015.
7. Bill Ruh (VP, software and analytics, GE), telephone interview with authors, June 4, 2014.
8. Raghu Krishnamoorthy (VP, executive development, and chief learning officer, GE), telephone interview with authors, March 9, 2015.
9. Fields interview.
10. Mike Giresi (CIO, Tory Burch), telephone interview with authors, February 10, 2015.
11. Klas Bendrik (CIO, Volvo Cars), interview with authors, May 5, 2014.
12. Mike Bracken (executive director of digital, U.K. government). interview with authors, August 26, 2014.
13. "Government Digital Strategy: December 2013" (policy paper), U.K. government website, https://www.gov.uk/government/publications/government-digital-strategy/government-digital-strategy.

14. Bracken interview

15. Giresi interview.

16. David Duffy (CEO, AIB), telephone interview with authors, November 3, 2015.

17. Bracken interview.

18. Dr. Hee Hwang (chief information officer and chief medical officer, Seoul National University Bundang Hospital), telephone interview with authors, January, 20, 2015.

19. Klevorn interview.

20. Giresi interview

21. Steve Perry (CDO, Visa Europe), interview with authors, August 14, 2014.

Chapter 9

1. Krischa Winright (chief information officer, Priority Health), telephone interview with authors, February 17, 2015; discussion in collaboration calls and meetings.

2. The ten skills evaluated and associated definitions came from Bob Johansen (distinguished fellow, Institute for the Future), *Leaders Make the Future: Ten New Leadership Skills for an Uncertain World* (Berrett-Koehler Publishers, 2009).

3. Johansen, *Leaders Make the Future.*

4. Johansen, *Leaders Make the Future.*

5. Johansen, *Leaders Make the Future.*

6. Roger Liew (chief technology officer, Orbitz Worldwide), telephone interview with authors, January 29, 2015.

7. Raghu Krishnamoorthy (VP, executive development, and chief learning officer, GE), telephone interview with authors, March 9, 2015.

8. Krishnamoorthy interview.

9. Bill Ruh (VP, GE Software), telephone interview with authors, June 4, 2014.

10. Krishnamoorthy interview.

11. Mike Bracken (executive director of digital, U.K. Government Cabinet Office), interview with authors, August 26, 2014.

12. Winright interview.

13. Arvind Gupta (innovation evangelist, information and technology head, Bharatiya Janata Party), telephone interview with authors, February 17, 2015.

Chapter 10

1. Innova Challenge is a BBVA initiative that aims to promote the open and collaborative culture between the bank and an active community of developers. http://www.centrodeinnovacionbbva.com/en/innovachallenge/home.

2. Marco Bressan (chairman, BBVA Data & Analytics), telephone interviews with authors, January 15, 2015, and March 20, 2015.

3. John Peretiatko (senior director, Zappos), telephone interview with authors, January 21, 2015.

4. Arvind Gupta (innovation evangelist, information and technology head, Bharatiya Janata Party), telephone interview with authors, February 17, 2015.

5. Casey Tolan, "Cities of the Future? Indian PM Pushes Plan for 100 'Smart Cities,'" CNN, July 18, 2014, http://www.cnn.com/2014/07/18/world/asia/india-modi-smart-cities/.

6. Linglong He (chief information officer, Quicken Loans), telephone interview with authors, July 21, 2014.

7. "Best Places to Work in IT, 2014 Employer Profile," *Computerworld*, http://www.computerworld.com/bestplaces/detail/1101.

8. He interview.

9. He interview.

10. He interview.

11. Raghu Krishnamoorthy (VP, executive development, and chief learning officer, GE), telephone interview with authors, March 9, 2015.

12. Krishnamoorthy interview.

13. Raghu Krishnamoorthy, "GE's Culture Challenge After Welch and Immelt," *Harvard Business Review* blog, January 26, 2015, https://hbr.org/2015/01/ges-culture-challenge-after-welch-and-immelt/.

14. Krishnamoorthy, "GE's Culture Challenge."

15. *Wikipedia,* "Anaximander," accessed June 1, 2015, http://en.wikipedia.org/wiki/Anaximander.

16. *Wikipedia.* "Anaximander."

17. Dean Crutchfield (chief information officer, Zebra Technologies), telephone interview with authors, September 28, 2014.

18. Mark Fields (chief executive officer, Ford), written research response to authors, March 18, 2015.

19. Marcy Klevorn (chief information officer, Ford), written research response to authors, March 18, 2015.

20. "MD Anderson Taps IBM Watson to Power 'Moon Shots' Misson," MD Anderson News Release, October 18, 2013, http://www.mdanderson.org/newsroom/news-releases/2013/ibm-watson-to-power-moon-shots-.html.

21. Eric Ries, *The Lean Startup: How Constant Innovation Creates Radically Successful Businesses* (New York: Portfolio Penguin, 2011).

22. Brian Burke and Gartner Inc., *Gamify* (Brookline: Bibliomotion, 2013).

23. "About Tesla Cars," Tesla website, accessed June 12, 2015, http://www.teslamotors.com/en_GB/about.

24. "About Google," Google website, accessed June 12, 2015, http://www.google.co.uk/about/company/.

INDEX

ACKNOWLEDGMENTS

The authors would like to thank the following people for their contributions to this work.

Heather Pemberton Levy, our project manager, writer, and internal editor. Without Heather's tireless efforts this and other Gartner books simply would not exist.

Our talented leaders at Bibliomotion, Inc.: Erika Heilman, Susan Lauzau, Jill Schoenhaut, and Shevaun Betzler.

Our many Gartner Research, Gartner EXP management, Research Board, analysts and other colleagues, whose support, research, ideas, insights, inspiration, collaboration, and reviews were vital to the creation of this work. Andrew Spender, Peter Sondergaard, Chris Thomas, Dave Melchers, John Kost, Diane Morello, Jorge Lopez, Dave Aron, Mary Mesaglio, Simon Mingay, Richard Hunter, Tina Nunno, Brian Burke, Frank Buytendijk, Patrick Meehan, Thilo Koslowski, John Lovelock, Hung LeHong, Jackie Fenn , Ken McGee, David Furlonger, Partha Iyengar, Robert Dye, Edward Gung, Nadia Cheraa, and many more.

Gartner's primary research staff who enable us to design and operate the CIO and CEO surveys used in this book: Angela Kreiter, Heather Keltz, Melissa Rossi Wood, Kathy Kenny.

For their skilled marketing and design of our book graphics: Monica Virag and Cynthia Miller.

Finally, of course, we wish to thank all of the government, business, and technology executive leaders who kindly provided their time and insights in research interviews that contributed to this book (though not all appear directly in the text).

Arjen Dorland, Arvind Gupta, Atif Rafiq, Bill Ruh, Bob Brese, Bob Johansen, Charles A. Thomas, Dana Deasy, David Duffy, Dario Scagliotti, David Smoley, Dean Crutchfield, Denise Clarke, Ed Marx, Eric Babolat, Fabrice Poussiere, Dr. Hee Hwang, Hidemi Harada-san, Jim Sappington, Joann Eisenhart, John Peretiatko, Keith Perry, Ken Daly, Klas Bendrik, Krischa Winright, Linglong He, Luis Saldana, Marco Bressan, Marcy Klevorn, Mark Fields, Mark Little, Maurice Levy, Mike Bracken, Mike Giresi, Nick Smither, Oliver Bussmann, Pete Goss, Raghu Krishnamoorthy, Rob Carter, Roger Liew, Russell Davies, Steve Perry, Terence Stacey, Timothy Schaefer, Tsukasa Makino-san, and Yvonne Schneider.

ABOUT THE AUTHORS

MARK RASKINO is a research vice president and Gartner Fellow in Gartner's Digital Business Leadership research team. He works primarily with CIOs and CEOs. His research covers business and technology trends and their implications for business strategy and technology management. Mark's research includes Gartner's Annual CEO Survey. An accomplished keynote speaker, Mark is also coauthor of *Mastering the Hype Cycle: How to Adopt the Right Innovation at the Right Time* (Harvard Business Review Press, 2008). He has been with Gartner for fifteen years. Previously, he was a senior IT manager at an airline.

GRAHAM WALLER is vice president research in Gartner's Digital Business Leadership research team. He works with CIOs and executive-level digital leaders with emphasis on contemporary leadership and realizing business value via technology. He is a coauthor of *The CIO Edge: Seven Leadership Skills You Need to Drive Results* (Harvard Business Review Press, 2010). Waller is also a coauthor of Gartner's 2014 CIO Agenda (*Taming the Digital Dragon*) and 2015 CIO Agenda (*Flipping to Digital Leadership*). He has been with Gartner for ten years, previously holding business and technology leadership positions with two Fortune 100 enterprises.